Warm Regards
Bob Pritikin

CHRIST WAS AN AD MAN

Miracle Ads for Big & Small Advertisers, Retailers and Entrepreneurs

by

Robert Pritikin

First edition published by Harbor
September 1980.

Second edition 1991 published previously
under title "Pritikin's Testament"
PRENTICE HALL
Division Simon & Schuster

Third edition, Christ Was An Ad Man, published 1997
BAY COURT PUBLISHERS
London - San Francisco
In the USA contact (415) 824-4458

ISBN 0-9659069-0-6

PRINTED IN THE UNITED STATES OF AMERICA

My very special thanks to some very special people who helped me put this book together: Jerry Gibbons, Tony Eglin, Bea Seidler, Eldon Braun, my son, Scott, and most especially, Marilyn Reynolds, whoever she may be.

DEDICATED TO MARILYN REYNOLDS

I am dedicating this book to a person I have never met. Before I randomly opened the San Francisco phone book to page 519, and plunged my finger onto the page over the name Marilyn Reynolds, I had never heard of the lady. Indeed, as this book goes to press, I have no concept of who she is, what she does, or how she thinks.

I am dedicating this book to Marilyn Reynolds because she is the anonymous person out there for whom I have been creating advertising for nearly a quarter of a century. In writing ads and commercials I never thought much of demographic profiles or market segmentations. But I have thought of a single person out there, a "Marilyn Reynolds," if you will.

Marilyn Reynolds, who are you? Are you a grande dame, or a child whose father gave you your very own phone? Are you an anti-vivisectionist? Are you a sex surrogate, shopkeeper, therapist, Avon Lady? Do you own a Cuisinart, do you subscribe to Lears, are you anorexic, are you pretty, are you plain, are you into hot tubs?

What color are you, Marilyn? Were you born in Corpus Christi? Are you a seamstress, stenographer, socialite, social worker? Maybe you are all those things.

Who is that lady? If anyone should know, I should. They've paid me hundreds of thousands of dollars to know who she is. I wrote the ads and commercials that persuaded her to buy General Electric coffee makers and Aqua Fem douching appliances and the Chevy Camaro. I sold her on Bufferin, Folger's Coffee, Spreckels Sugar, Olds Cutlass. I even sold that lady a condominium in Tahoe. But who is she?

Dear "Marilyn Reynolds," whoever you are. When this book is published, I intend to phone you. I will tell you, "Marilyn Reynolds, my name is Bob Pritikin and I dedicated my book to you." I will then invite you to lunch, and I hope you will accept. Because I owe you my thanks.

FOREWORD

by
JERRY GIBBONS

SENIOR VICE PRESIDENT,
AMERICAN ASSOCIATION OF ADVERTISING AGENCIES

There I was in the men's room at the Park Hyatt Hotel in Washington D.C. The gentleman at the urinal to my left was enraged. "Those bastards," he seethed, "that's going to cost them another five million dollars."

We were taking a break from the morning meeting of the American Association of Advertising Agencies' National Board. One of the joys of being on this prestigious panel is that it brought me into personal contact with some of the advertising giants of our time. This includes Bob Jacoby, Chairman of Ted Bates Advertising, who was exercised over a phone call he had just received from London.

Bob Jacoby is one among an elite group of advertising innovators and advertising legends I was privileged to know as a result of my activities in professional advertising organizations throughout the U.S. As a board member of the national 4-As and as President of the San Francisco Advertising Club and The Society of Communicating Arts I encountered the monoliths of marketing and advertising.

Advertising on our planet was forever changed by the likes of Bob Jacoby and other gifted communicators such as Bill Bernbach, David Ogilvey, Hal Riney, Pat Gallagher and John O'Toole. Other luminaries in the advertising world whose lights shined with a higher wattage were Ned Doyle, Max Dane, Paul Kaye, Al Wolfe, Barry Loughrane, Bob Kuperman, Neil O'Conner, Mike Koelker, Helmut Krone, Bob Levenson, Monty McKiney, Jerry Siano, Kieth Reinhard, Phil Joanue, Burtch Drake and John Mercer. What a joy it was to know and work with these creative pioneers. But one talent in particular, personifies the inventive skills and derring-do of them all. He is the volcanic talent who became my partner in the San Francisco based advertising agency, Pritikin & Gibbons Communications—Bob Pritikin.

It was at my urgings that Bob consented to share his unique formulas for creative innovation and advertising cost efficiencies in this book, Christ Was An Ad Man.

Jerry L. Gibbons

TABLE OF CONTENTS

INTRODUCTION

GOD IS THE CLIENT

The advertising business is a trinity: client, agency, and media. The client, of course, is god. And so it has been ever since the days of the first great ad man—Jesus Christ.

The client calls the shots, the advertising agency develops the message, and the media carry the message to the people.

Most good advertising messages can be condensed into a few words, called selling propositions or slogans. The best slogans embody the essence of the full message; they are catchy, memorable and enduring. Historically, brilliant slogans such as "Better Buy Birdseye," "There's a Ford in Your Future," "Good to the Last Drop," and "A Little Dab'll Do You" have a consumer life expectancy of years, even decades.

Of all the slogans created throughout the history of selling, one alone stands above all others for its brilliant phrasing, its roll-off-the-tongue memorability, its glorious brevity (one should test all slogans as to how well they function on outdoor billboards), its relevancy to the product, its persuasive impact and its endurability. Lord, it's been a household phrase for hundreds of years: DO UNTO OTHERS AS YOU WOULD HAVE OTHERS DO UNTO YOU.

Christ was indeed a brilliant ad man, an entire advertising agency unto himself. And he had a tough sell—a new idea for which there was no record of success against a formidable competitor, the entire Roman Empire. But he had a very strong selling proposition—the best: His product was *new,* and it certainly was *amazing*. Reflect on all those red stars on detergent boxes that scream AMAZING! NEW! And he had *miracles*. Though advertising successors have introduced "miracles," too—miracle drugs, miracle gravies, miracle detergents—no one, of course, has ever matched the true miracles of Christ.

Twentieth-century broadcast and print media bombard us with unrelenting fervor, but Christ depended upon a much more effective, albeit simpler media network: He engaged a staff of twelve dedicated and talented gentlemen to broadcast his message throughout the land. And to this day, there is no more effective means of advertising than word-of-mouth advertising.

A great advertising campaign never happened without a great client behind it. Way back on September 17, 1951 David Ogilvy created the innovative Hathaway Shirt eyepatch campaign, but it was his client, Ellerton Jette, whose trust and courage inspired it. Bill Bernbach wrote the first words and pictures for the breakthrough Volkswagen campaign, with its disarming candor which dared to headline the auto as a "lemon," but it was the gutsy client who said *go!* When I pleaded with the Fuller Paint Company to engage the radio medium instead of the print medium to sell "color," it was not I but clearly the client who had the most to lose if it didn't work.

The client is god. Often a false one, but sometimes there's a real one out there—to support and inspire and encourage those few talents who would go to the Cross on his behalf.

Christ had such a client.

It is my hope that this little book will offer you—the small merchant, the big merchant, the manufacturer of goods and dispenser of services, the beginning copywriter, the job-seeker enamored of mass communications and the ultimate consumer—insights and revelations about those miracle advertising campaigns that beat the pants off their competitors.

This book is about how to produce breakthroughs and advertising miracles. Christ knows, it's not easy.

Or is it—if you just know how?

CHAPTER I

FALSE PROPHETS AND THE ODD-VERTISING AGENCY

hame, shame, everybody knows your name—you are the client!

By and large, the slick, multi-tiered computerized advertising agency is an octopus—out of water, falling out of a tree, its departmental arms flailing sloppily all over the place.

Agency presidents, smiling through sinister eyes, waltz you about. Insufferable forty-year-old teen-age account executives stand up like automatons around shiny conference tables mouthing sophomoric ideas about how you should run your own business. Copywriters suggesting cutesy-pie slogans that should make grown men puke. Art directors, mesmerized by their computer screens, think little words floating in yards of white space will make effective billboard advertising. Pour in your dollars, you fools! There's a machine out there as hungry as it is inept, run by children, administered by fear, and sometimes dedicated to the proposition that *you* can be propositioned.

Withdraw now. Your money is ticking away. You pay for the hundred conference reports, the Xerox copies, the in-house jabber, the stolen paper clips, the fancy lunch the account executive buys. You pay for all the ill-advised ideas as you smile at the children who write them. And finally, you surrender—exhausted, bitter, spent, infuriated, frustrated, nauseated. You surrender because there is no more time: The space is bought, the ads must run.

Ad executives don't miss deadlines. But all too often, they just miss the whole point.

They miss because advertising agencies are not heavily populated with advertising people. There are very few *advertising* people in the world. Most people engaged in advertising could just as well be telephone people or transportation people or software people or wholesale Naugahyde people. Almost nobody in the advertising business is an advertising person. Beware of the false prophets. When you find the real prophets, the *real* profits will follow.

Advertising is intended to be the art of mass communication. Art is discipline, but it's visceral, too. You have to feel. A great salesman sells with his heart as well as his head. And the consumer must buy what the salesman *says* before he buys what he *sells*. And the buying decision, more often than not, is made on the basis of feelings. It just "feels" right.

Thus, an ad man creating a television commercial must feel what will reach out through a TV tube and embrace and cajole and persuade. In print media, he must know the power of words, and in radio, the power of a pause. Few people in any advertising agency understand or feel the secret idiom of persuasion. Those few who do are the ones who, if you can find them and get them assigned to your account, could make your company rich and you a hero.

People who work for an advertising agency can be in any one of a dozen job categories ranging from the president's waitress, often called his secretary; to a copywriter, some who indeed *copy* what they write; to a production manager producing tantrums; to a mailboy, usually an upcoming agency president; to some pedantic-twerp research director; to an art director (many rush home at night to paint sailboats and farmhouses); to an account executive, with crisp collars and sweaty armpits; to the agency broadcast producer, who duplicates the function of an outside hired producer and whose questionable purpose is exceeded only by the Stepin Fetchit men's room attendant whisk-brooming imaginary dust from your shoulder with one hand while extending the other for a tip.

These are some of the ad folks in the odd-vertising agency, but there are others, too—the sweet, lovely, uncorrupted, talented souls who could later turn into the aforementioned. If you are a client and can engage them before their sad metamorphosis, you have a solid resource. If you can find them after they have been withered, weathered, and wrenched—after they have withdrawn from all the nincompoopery; after they have seasoned and had a rebirth to logic and reality—you will have found a treasure trove of sagacity and experience and talent that can quickly and effortlessly produce great insights, the fuel for great advertising.

It is not my intention in this chapter to discredit all advertising agencies. Only some. There are some smaller, inspired agencies staffed by seasoned professionals who deplore waste, mediocrity and role-playing as much as you do. And there are monolithic agencies, employing thousands of people, which have pockets of talent and which sometimes train their clients to expect and demand brilliance and excellence with the same fervor that they train their people to deliver it.

There are options for the advertiser other than that of simply engaging the expensive services of a departmentalized advertising agency. Such options include doing it yourself and saving a bundle, engaging the services of a one or two-person operation with proven credentials, or opening your own in-house agency.

Such alternatives could better satisfy the demands of your business and the yearnings inside yourself to associate with great advertising or, at the very least, competent advertising produced in the fastest time at the lowest cost. But should you, for countless practical reasons, elect to join or appoint an advertising agency, I hope you will encourage your agency to heed some of the commandments and dogmas in the pages to follow. You will learn formulas that are simple beyond your imaginings, cost-saving techniques that will quadruple the effectiveness of your advertising budget, however big or small.

Please don't take this light book *too* lightly. Between the giggles is more than a quarter-century of advertising agency experience. I have moved from mailboy to agency president; from nervous-kid-out-of-the-mail-room, rosy-cheeked and raring to go, to ad agency expatriate. I have seen grown men faint behind conference tables, too terrified to open their mouths and recite their litany of clichés to a prospective client whose advertising budget could "make the agency." I have seen a creative director race into the office of a lady copywriter and slug her in the snoot. I have seen Dale Zaret, a Los Angeles copy chief, send an insolent art director crashing through a second-story window. I have seen an account executive writhing in pain on the floor of his office—a cardiac arrest, engendered by the stress of his job and the tensions of the day. I have known five suicides of grown men and women so frustrated by one of the world's most curious and demanding businesses that they took what they thought was the only way out.

And I have made mistakes—ads and campaigns, that never hit the mark. I bear secret scars of humiliation at having persuaded clients to underwrite indulgent, frivolous or even devious campaigns that may have looked good in my portfolio but not have been best for their sales—or my conscience. But my guilt now is bearable because I reflect on my youth at the time, my naiveté, my former bravado. And I will still make misjudgments and mistakes, but when I do my client will share the responsibility. Because, if the idea is monumental, we will go hand in hand with the calculated risk. And if it fails—so be it. But if it doesn't—watch out!

Those advertising concepts that achieve heroic results are those for which there is no precedent. Pretesting them before they are exposed in the media invariably guarantees their doom. Consumer panels recoil and withdraw from new ideas, and so do consumers on first exposure of a breathtaking departure in the media.

An advertising counsel acquainted with this phenomenon will educate his client to expect an initial lethargic or even negative response—before the sea parts open and the sales pour in. Advertising agencies that rely heavily on pretesting ideas rarely produce the miracles. A great conviction never came from a committee, an inspired campaign has never been born from a conference table free-for-all. Those new, startling, fresh ideas that had never been thought before are born from secret layers deep beneath the conscious—inside those rare people who dare to grope in the dark for glimmers of light.

But when that pinpoint of light explodes in a vision, *that's* when the real test begins, the test of persistence. How many brilliant ideas have gathered dust in agency files because the agency clods wouldn't persist in selling them to their clients? Bruce Campbell, who produced the film classic, *Johnny Got His Gun,* handed me a credo on persistence:

NOTHING IN THE WORLD
CAN TAKE THE PLACE OF PERSISTENCE.

TALENT WILL NOT;
NOTHING IS MORE COMMON THAN
UNSUCCESSFUL MEN WITH TALENT.

GENIUS WILL NOT;
UNREWARDED GENIUS IS
ALMOST A PROVERB.

EDUCATION WILL NOT;
THE WORLD IS FULL
OF EDUCATED DERELICTS.

PERSISTENCE AND DETERMINATION
ALONE ARE OMNIPOTENT.

CHAPTER II

JESUS SAVES. YOU CAN TOO— ON AD COSTS

Last year nearly $200 billion was spent in the United States on advertising products and services in broadcast and print. Most of the clients who underwrote that massive cost were gypped. If they all knew what you will find out in this book, billions of dollars would have been saved.

Few got the attention, readership and results from their ads that they paid for. Why? Because all too often the content of the ads was inane; the layouts were ill-advised; the selling ideas were wrong; the media choice was ill-considered; and the advertising agencies were inattentive, uninspired or in many cases simply didn't have the wherewithal in talent and marketing sophistication to do the job.

If you are a client, this book will give you new attitudes and clear formulas to ensure that your dollars spent on outdoor billboards, radio commercials, small and big-space newspaper and magazine ads, television commercials, direct mail, doorstep fliers, public relations, trade ads, merchandising displays, sky-writing and even whisper campaigns are spent with such cost efficiency and brilliance that, where your competitor gets fifty cents return on his advertising dollar, you will get two dollars back in sales results.

Let's consider a regional advertiser spending $5 million-plus per year to push his product. Now in the big time, he has engaged the services of a fully departmentalized advertising agency to handle his account. On an organizational chart, the client is reassured that the full resources of the agency are to be pressed against his marketing objectives. Indeed, those resources will probably be expected to tell him what his marketing objectives are in the first place—a responsibility that, before the advertising agency decided to take on everything, was logically in the exclusive domain of the client.

Now a bunch of mailboy graduates, secretaries in Reeboks, anorexic media buyers, anti-establishment writers, art directors who can't draw, research directors with computer printout minds and account executives drawn from central casting convene around a conference table at a huge aggregate hourly wage to cook up a multimillion-dollar plan for some potato chip company or fast food chain or manufacturer of dry goods or hard goods or what have you. Almost never have the people attempting these decisions worked in the business they were engaged to promote. Indeed, few if any have ever been in *any* business save their experience in the effete, elite advertising agency business. The evidence will show that few clients can endure their appointed agency for more than a few years at most, moving on to another agency for another few years of outrage until the next desperate move.

There are advertisers spending upwards of ten million each year, their principal communication to the outside world being a handful of thirty-second television commercials. In support of this apparently simple effort is a battery of high-priced know-it-alls including the closeted copywriter who came up with the idea and is expected to follow through on its execution. His total time spent on the creative project could be just a couple of days, to which the agency adds interminable meetings, memos, call reports, status reports, market research, advertising research, media research and mind-boggling machinations in order to justify profits of hundreds of thousands of dollars in media commissions.

To compound the dilemma, the advertiser who underwrites this enormous cost delegates his decisions to a corporate underling who probably flunked all his job interviews with advertising agencies and was therefore obliged to take a lower-paying job on the client side.

In a sizable company, top management often refers the advertising responsibilities to a youthful Harvard Business School type hot dog who rarely has any more practical knowledge and working business experience than the ad agency "specialists" he depends upon. Usually, this blind-leading-the-blind association leads to trouble.

It is astonishing that the chairman of the board or the president of those companies that engage advertising agencies do not take on more direct personal control and responsibility for the advertising function. It is often one of their major operating expenses; it defines the image of their products or services to the outside world; it is frequently the most potent tool for increasing sales and profits; and, all things considered, it is much more fun than haggling with stockholders.

But more important than all of the aforementioned, it is the people in top management—the chairman, the president, the sales manager—who have the most sensitive visceral feeling for their company and its products. They also have the proven leadership capacity as well as the authority and guts to say, "Let's do advertising that is innovative, penetrating, persuasive and incisive, and goddammit, if it doesn't work I will take the responsibility." Few product managers or advertising managers or underlings would ever say that.

The simple truth is that the advertising business is utterly simple. If one can see through the maze of memos; if one can hear through the din of advertisingese chatter and the eternal internal bickering; if one can feel through the insensitive, robotic reliance on demographic studies, consumer profiles, and market reports—then one uncovers the simple truth that a great ad or lasting campaign is usually born from the insights of a single human being, who, like a great author or painter or inventor, can find the essence; understand the gestalt; and then give his creation a life of its own. Given some basic marketing input, this advertising talent can quickly and effortlessly conjure up an entire advertising program that will beat the pants off of any competitor.

Open any newspaper. Find a page with lots of ads. You will note that many small ads have twice the impact and visibility of the big ads next to them. You should also know that newspaper space is sold by the column inch. There are techniques that, if applied with religious discipline, can ensure that a five-inch ad will get the same attention and readership as a ten-inch ad. If there is an average readership for a certain product category in a ten-inch ad, and if that same readership can be achieved in a five-inch ad, then it follows that the advertiser with the five-inch ad is getting twice the value for his dollars. If that advertiser spends $10,000, he actually has an effective advertising budget of $20,000.

Thus, an advertiser with a $100,000 ad budget can wage holy hell against a competitor spending $200,000 if he carefully follows a few simple techniques. If you can't outspend your competitor, outfox him. Advertising dollars are like no other dollars, whether you're General Motors or the 4-Star Gift Shoppe, because an advertising dollar can be worth fifty cents or worth ten cents. Or worth ten dollars. Every ad, in every product category, has an *average* expected readership. Every radio and TV commercial, in every product category, has an *average* expected "attention value." If you are matching your competitor's advertising dollars but your program is so skillful as to demand twice the attention and persuasion, you are in an enviable position. Consider cutting your advertising budget in half or consider maintaining your present budget level—and put your competition in a most defensive situation.

If one spends a dollar on advertising, one should expect that *at least* a dollar profit is returned. That dollar profit would then cover the cost of the advertising, and nothing gained, nothing lost. But to break even is not the intended function of advertising dollars. Their ideal purpose, of course, is to generate revenue over and above the advertising costs and the costs of dispensing the products and services. Yet few advertisers have even the vaguest idea of any positive correlation between their dollars spent in print or in broadcasting and increased profits.

Probably the only medium that can accurately assess this concern is the medium of direct-response advertising, which is the domain of coupon ads; direct mail with return envelopes; catalogs with 800 numbers; the world-wide web; and occasionally broadcast advertising that monitors phone responses and write-in requests. By and large, however, advertisers have no proof that their advertising is reaching and persuading—save a few comments from friends or a rare letter from a consumer which, if favorable, is always sent to the top office.

Sometimes the greatest service an advertising agency can provide its client is to recommend he stop consumer advertising altogether and instead plow the money into new product development or public relations or a blockbuster program directed to the trade or a strengthened sales force. Though few agencies would sacrifice their commissions by making such a pragmatic recommendation, ad men could save their clients a lot of money if they would do unto others as they would have others do unto them. I shudder to think how many tens of millions would be saved if the ad men spent as much time and energy saving their clients' dollars as they do saving their own asses.

CHAPTER III

JESUS WENT DOOR TO DOOR

A great salesman hones his craft through experience, eye to eye with his prospects. He sells more with his heart than with his head; he views his prospect not as a prey but as a partner; he believes in every word he says and in everything he sells; he speaks the truth and offers proof; he inspires. Such was the salesman Jesus as he went village to village, door to door.

A good salesman not only excites the prospect but closes the sale. Rarely does an ad make a good pitch. That is because the ad men who write them don't know how to close a sale. A hot headline will get attention, but the bottom line is whether the sale is closed.

Many college and university advertising courses have intern programs in which promising students spend their summers in a real, live ad agency. The little darlings would be far better initiated into the real principles of advertising were they sent out to hustle Avon products or Fuller Brushes door to door. Then they would learn the art of selling instead of the art of snowing, and they would discover that no amount of razzle-dazzle and gimmickry can be justified if it doesn't result in a sale. Let them just try the kind of nonsense sloganeering on the doorstep, face to face with the prospect, that their agency mentors foist on the public through print and broadcast advertising, and they would find the door slammed loudly in their faces.

The salesmen of the electronic airwaves in particular live cloistered lives. While legions of their potential customers, incensed at their insipid drivel, turn the dials or turn the sets off completely, they keep rattling on inside their electronic boxes. They simply don't know that advertising should be selling, pure and simple. How rare is that ad or commercial that is pure and simple, that looks you in the eye, on a one-to-one basis, and honestly persuades you to make a purchase.

I first learned my craft on the doorsteps. I was seven years old, my white *Liberty* magazine bag slung across my shoulders, working the trailer park in Corpus Christi, Texas. Did I say trailer park? It was a ghetto of overturned cars housing entire families, replete with screaming babies, barking, biting dogs and wailing cats. Many of the infants had their own bedrooms, orange crates displaying the same end labels I have seen merchandised in a chic shop on San Francisco's Pier 39 called Orange Crate Art. It was during these prepubescent years that I learned the art of one-to-one selling. Sadly, I also learned the sham of selling what nobody wanted, nobody needed and nobody could afford.

I will spare you many details of my ensuing years through high school and college in Los Angeles, where the family finally settled, except to say that every job I had, from inventing and publishing the first teen-age magazine to hawking light bulbs, brushes, modeling courses and subscriptions door to door, was a preordination into my future career in advertising. Indeed, were I to be asked for my principal credential as an effective advertising man, I'd answer that it was my experience working for Big Red Mat Newman as a door to door solicitor.

Big Red was a great, slobbering, yiddisha pussycat who drove around in a monster station wagon, picking up his teen-age employees on street corners like a modern-day Fagin and training them to bilk the unwary for monthly subscriptions to the *Los Angeles Herald Express*. I was among his flock of about fifteen boys who squeezed into his station wagon every day after high school and college to be raced off to such bedroom communities as Tarzana, Happy Valley, San Pedro, and Oxnard. I don't recall my exact commission per subscription sold, but I do remember that, while in high school, my hourly income was between five and ten dollars when the minimum wage hovered around a dollar.

Among the teen-aged ragamuffins who worked the streets was Joe Boker—I presume the same Joe Boker who, I have since read, married and divorced the late Christina Onassis; famed Hollywood hair stylist Gene Shecove, seen plugging VO5 on national TV; Mark Damon, formerly Mark Harris and before that Al Herskowitz, who became an internationally acclaimed B movie star with the name, Mark Damon and is now one of Hollywood's legendary producers; Mo Ostrofksy, now Morris Ostin, former president and chairman of the board of Warner Brothers Records; Mike Emory, formerly Myron Elfinbine, who is the renowned attorney specialist in advertising and show biz law; and the Academy Award-winning superstar Joel Katz, now Joel Grey; plus other names, either too prominent to mention or too obscure to remember, who were mesmerized, intimidated and otherwise motivated to get out on the streets and break their butts to sell the *Los Angeles Herald Express*.

Most of our subscription sales did not endure for much more than a month, and some of the boys wondered why their commissions actually exceeded the cost of the first month's subscription. It became clear to some of us, even in those tender years, that we were *not* selling subscriptions but rather quick circulation increases which could affect advertising rates.

The competition among the teen-aged solicitors was fierce, inspiring sometimes bizarre behavior. Those of us, myself included, who wore high school letterman sweaters, had a distinct advantage. I wore my high school sweater at the doorsteps until I was well into college and no one ever questioned my more advanced years.

"Hi," I would say. "Has anyone spoken to you about the work my brother and I are doing in the neighborhood?"

This was, in fact, a highly sophisticated opener, not unlike the first line of an effective television or radio commercial. A pleasant, innocent question can sometimes make for a good headline. The reader or listener, even on a doorstep, may have only one recourse: to answer the question. In the case of my doorstep prey, it would have to be, "What work?"

The prospective buyer had now been placed in a vulnerable situation. By simply asking the question "What work?" he or she had to listen to my answer, which at long last would wind and wend itself into a selling proposition. To heighten the prospect's commitment to listening carefully, I would continue, "Are you *sure* nobody spoke to you yesterday or today about the work my brother and I are doing?" To which the prospect would implore, "Now what work?" And the floor would be mine, with little chance of interruption.

My presentation was calculated to thoroughly confuse the prospect, but eventually he or she would extract out of the jumble of words and frenzied excitement the fact that I could get a job as an assistant manager in charge of *Herald Express* delivery boys if I could prove I had the support of my neighbors by acquiring fifty one-month-only subscriptions. It was a curious and spurious logic which I do not recall was ever challenged.

On a good day, I could sell one out of two doors I knocked on. However, a good day depended, first, on the neighborhood. The best selling areas were known as "cream territory" (in the ad biz, known as "prime market area"), and the best houses, for reasons unknown, were back houses (prime market target). Wherever there was a smaller house at the rear of a larger house, that house was certain to be occupied by a very soft touch who would provide not only a subscription order but on occasions a *schtup,* which some of my readers will recognize as a sexual favor.

Some of us lost all propriety on the doorsteps and performed the most outlandish antics. One of my favorites was to ring the bell and then stand on my hands, wearing my gymnast letterman's sweater from L.A. High. Upon opening the door, the prospect would discover me balanced upside down. I would launch into my presentation as if this were a perfectly normal posture for a young man selling subscriptions door-to-door. On occasion, the astonished or terrified prospect would promptly slam the door on my upside-down face, but generally this attention-getting device worked just fine—like a good headline.

The *tour de force* of my doorstep inventions was the palsied-hand routine. My right hand would grip fifty or more subscription forms, shaking in a back-and-forth staccato rhythm from the moment the prospect opened the door until, well into my sales pitch, they would fly out of my hand and scatter on the floor of her entrance hall. I would profusely apologize as the confounded lady of the house kneeled down to retrieve the cards. While palsy of the hand is a malady of more advanced years, no one ever questioned the legitimacy of my infirmity. The ploy invariably resulted in a subscription sale, or at the very least provided me with a secret chuckle to relieve the routine of my selling day.

One of my fellow solicitors was even more adventuresome. I believe his name was Bill Engle, the very Bill Engle who pulled out his pud on the doorsteps. On occasion, when I completed all the houses on my side of the street, I would join my partner on the opposite side while he completed his. Engle's idea of rollicking amusement was to reach into his liningless pocket and withdraw his private. It was not his intention to make the prospect privy to his playful exhibitionism, but he would skillfully alert *me* by opening his hand, positioned tightly at his hip, and slyly displaying his appendage, all the while rattling on to the lady about his job opportunity with the *Herald Express*. While Engle may have outdone even my doorstep antic in sheer derring-do, I feel mine would have scored higher on the creative scale.

We were indeed a madcap crew, racing about greater Los Angeles under the tutelage of Big Red, whose toothless grin and gutter mouth taught me as much about selling as any instructor I've ever known. It was selling for quick bucks, motivated by the spirit of fun and the willingness to try anything to make a sale. It was selling as primitive, as gutsy, as intuitive, as sophisticated as any in the world. And it was invaluable training for a career in advertising because, unlike selling in a retail store, where the customer is mentally set to buy and requests help and information from the salesman, this kind of selling was an intrusion, an interruption, pushing a product for which no buying interest had been first expressed. That is precisely the characteristic of all advertisements. Because they appear unannounced, uninvited, and often sell products or services that are perceived as unneeded, the highest level of skill and persuasion is needed to crack the ice and make the sale.

If those legions of advertising copywriters, with their pompous pap and silly slogans and innocuous ideas, could have first apprenticed with someone like Big Red Mat Newman, I can only guess how much more Arrid Extra Dry, Pepto-Bismol, Nyquil, Minute Rice, Spic and Span, Hormel Chili, Star-Kist Tuna, Gallo Wine, Pontiac Firebirds, Allstate premiums, or Delta flights to Florida they'd be selling through print and broadcast advertising.

Many advertisers and their agency counsels take a far too casual approach to problem solving, standing around much of the time with their hands in their pockets. Perhaps like Engle they should reach down and dig a little deeper, and pull something out. Anything!

CHAPTER IV

THE NOT-SO-IMMACULATE CONCEPTION

The *concept* of an ad or an advertising campaign is the selling proposition. A good ad or ad campaign must have a concept. A good concept must have "balls"; or "chutzpah"; or "insight"; or "inspiration." The concept of an ad can be its "hook" or "the schtick" or "the angle" or "the gimmick" or "the twist" or "the relevancy" or "the sheer bravado." Or the "AMAZING, NEW!"

Sometimes the basic concept is *love*, as we shall see. But the best concept is the AMAZING, NEW!

It is often the advertising agency that is expected to come up with the AMAZING, NEW. But clearly this is absurd. How can an ad agency come up with a new Sony pocket videocamera, after all—or a new fuel-saving vehicle or a safe cigarette or a new instrument for banking? How can an ad agency, in fact, come up with *any* substantive innovation for a product or service?

Many dispensers of services or goods do not take new product research seriously, though in fact new and improved products and services should be the life blood of an organization's marketing plans. But they depend instead upon their advertising counsels to conjure up the illusion of newness by giving the advertising for their tired old products a new twist.

Many years ago, before Folger's Coffee was absorbed by the conglomnivorous Proctor & Gamble, I performed just such an improbity for Instant Folger's Coffee. Millions of coffee drinkers would be persuaded that Folger's had developed an AMAZING, NEW food-processing skill that made Instant Folger's indistinguishable in taste from fresh-brewed ground coffee. In point of fact, Folger's had done essentially nothing to change their product.

Those were the days when instant coffee *really* had a bad image—so bad, in fact, that the Folger's people would not even advertise their instant and ground coffee in the same ad. Though their instant was the higher profit item, as coffee traditionalists they secretly regarded it as ersatz and a stepchild. Both Jim and Peter Folger were professional coffee tasters, and, of course, they could at once perceive the difference in any blind tasting.

But it was my conviction that the average palate was not as discerning as the Folger brothers, so I set out to conduct my own horseback survey. I set up my experimental kitchen in my advertising office, inviting the entire staff one by one to sip from six numbered cups on my desk. Three cups contained instant coffee; three, ground coffee. I informed the testees (curious word) that they were to sip and savor and then decide which was instant and which was fresh-brewed ground. Before the test, each taster professed confidence that he or she could determine which was which.

After some fifteen people took the taste test, it was clear there was no pattern of accuracy; instead, there was total confusion as to which was which. Knowing that a panel of ad men and women may have been atypical samples—what with their olfactories numbed from tobacco tar and martinis—I decided to extend my experiment to a wider cross section. But to my delight, even most of my abstentious friends were unable to accurately isolate the instant coffee flavor from the ground coffee flavor. Hence was born the "breakthrough":

PRESENTING THE WORLD'S FIRST INSTANT COFFEE PROVED TO TASTE AS GOOD AS GROUND!

The word NEW was added to each label. Was it the product that was new—or merely the advertising?

To support this AMAZING, NEW concept a series of carefully controlled tests were held in church and community meeting halls. An independent research group presented hundreds of volunteers with steaming cups of coffee, both instant and ground. Between sips they were encouraged to clear their palates with water and bland crackers. As expected, there was a very high frequency of inaccuracy as they tried to determine which was which.

Folger's preempted all of their competitors with their dramatic claim, and while any competing brand could have proved the same point, Folger's was the first, and their sales skyrocketed as they inundated billboards, television, radio, newsprint and magazine ads with their new, legally supportable claim, GOOD

AS GROUND—three easy monosyllables, that for Instant Folger's Coffee became good as gold.

There's an AMAZING, NEW or at least an implied AMAZING, NEW in almost every product. Ideally, the manufacturer, not the advertising, should provide the new ingredient. When I visited the Pureta Sausage Company in Sacramento, California, I realized it would have to be the advertising, not the product, that would create a sense of excitement and newness.

"What's so special about your frankfurters?" I asked the weenie president. "Nothing," he answered. "All hot dogs are pretty much the same."

"Now, there must be something, however miniscule a difference, that makes a Pureta frank special or better than others," I pressed on.

"No, they're all the same," insisted the hot dog head.

In spite of the Pureta president's insistence that theirs was an ordinary hot dog, I was determined to come up with something special, something new.

I took the factory tour. I saw the cow come in the front door and observed all the steps in between until it was shipped out the back door as a package of weenies. There had to be a new idea hiding in the hot dog, I knew; there just had to be.

"There must be something, anything, that makes your product different," I implored the client, "the spices, the grinding, the packaging, *anything*."

"No. We run a clean plant, we use good beef, but all franks are really the same." He was plainly growing uneasy at my persistence.

"Well, does the whole cow go into the frankfurters?"

He assured me it did except for some of the scuzzy parts.

"Do you mean including the New York cuts, the market steaks, the T-bone steaks?"

"If we were to pull out those cuts, it would take more time and cost us more in production."

The not-so-immaculate conception worked its way out of the underpinnings of my subconscious and into the forefront of my advertising brain. "That's IT!" I screamed to my secret self.

THERE'S T-BONE STEAK IN EVERY FRANK!

I shook the president's hand. "Thank you for your time. The tour was fascinating." I returned to San Francisco to implement my new blockbuster concept.

The presentation a week later went just fine, and a few weeks thereafter highway billboards proclaimed PURETA—THERE'S T-BONE STEAK IN EVERY FRANK. A chorus of voices sang the slogan on radio, newspaper ads reasserted the theme, as did grocery store shelf strips—the whole, as they say, ball of wax. A new campaign was born. The theme did not state in so many words AMAZING, NEW, but the magic words were substantially implied. Sales went up, up, up.

Perhaps my most stunning victory in uncovering the AMAZING, NEW occurred when I was on an assignment for Leslie Salt. My relationship with the client began with the inevitable, "What's so special about Leslie Salt?" And the inevitable reply was, "Nothing; all salt is exactly the same."

I told the client I didn't believe it.

He tried vigorously to reassure me that all salt—his, Morton, all the others—was exactly the same, a colorless or white crystalline solid, chiefly sodium chloride, and that "Salt is salt, period."

Later I sat frustrated in my office before the round blue Morton box and the round red Leslie box. I poured little mounds of salt on the conference table. I touched, stared, and tasted. The client was right; the two brands of salt were identical.

Still, there *had* to be a difference. Or at least there had to be something special about generic salt that Leslie could preempt as its very own, to create some excitement and the illusion of newness.

I borrowed a magnifying glass from an art director. I studied Leslie. I studied Morton. Zazzzaaammm! There WAS a difference! Leslie salt crystals were *smaller* than Morton.

But why, I wondered, did the client conceal this tiny but monumental difference from me? Perhaps he didn't even know himself, and if he did he probably thought: So what?

"Did you know that your salt crystals are smaller than Morton salt crystals?" I asked him.

"They are?" he said. "So what?"

Later, he admitted that Leslie perhaps did indeed grind its salt a tad smaller than did competing brands. But he was incredulous when I told him that imperceptible difference could translate into a consumer benefit.

A pound of Leslie salt, I theorized, provided at least a million extra crystals in every box. These smaller crystals would permit the salt to pour faster and easier, with less clogging, from the shaker. As a result, with Leslie Salt you truly got a better shake. A better shake? That's IT! *You get a better shake with Leslie Salt!*

**YOU GET A BETTER SHAKE
WITH LESLIE SALT!**

I rushed the concept into a musical production orchestrated with a mambo beat and punctuated with the rhythmic sound of maracas—except it was the sound of salt shaking in the Leslie box.

A perky female voice sang, "You get a better shake, better shake, you get a better shake with Leslie Salt!" An announcer, speaking over an instrumental background, explained all the reasons why "You get a better shake with Leslie Salt."

I adapted the radio music for an audition presentation in which I visually proved that Leslie poured better and faster than the one that "pours when it rains." Two hourglasses, one containing Leslie salt, the other, Morton salt, were placed before the television cameras. At the word *Go!* the hourglasses were turned upside down and the race began. Leslie, of course, because of its smaller crystals, was the winner.

If you don't recall viewing this commercial on television or hearing the musical version on radio, it is because the client never bought the idea. Instead, he opted for an innocuous, noncompetitive advertising approach that would ensure the continued relative obscurity of his product. So I herewith offer the concept and the slogan to any table salt producer who may wish to turn a knob in his salt factory to reduce the crystal size, thereby increasing his competitive advantage with a NEW concept for salt. The campaign is yours, whoever you may be. Take it, please be my guest.

While the best concept may be the AMAZING, NEW—particularly if it is the product, not the advertising, that is new—there are other concepts. As I said at the beginning, sometimes the best one is love.

Critics of advertising should remind themselves that ads and commercials sell products other than Preparation H and Crest and Gilbey's gin. But before they get too sanctimonious, they should remember that when their bottoms itch and their teeth start to decay and their souls need an escape, it's nice to know there *is* Preparation H with its soothing analgesic and Crest toothpaste with fluoride and Gilbey's gin to send them off to their meanderings. Perhaps there are not-so-immaculate selling conceptions supporting such products; but, when you must advertise for muscular dystrophy or the Red Cross or blind babies or AIDS victims, or the dying whales or the threatened environment, on the other hand, you must muster love. Suddenly, the same techniques and skills used to develop the not-so-immaculate conception become *very* immaculate indeed.

Michael McClosky, the former executive director of the Sierra Club, sent his emissary to call on me. Theirs was a noble purpose: to save the entire world. It seemed that the disappearance of a few zillion microscopic creatures burrowing in the mud was threatening the very existence of man. I was both stunned at the impending biocide, albeit eons would have to pass, and thrilled with the idea of saving all life on our planet.

My partner Jerry Gibbons and I met with two scientists in a hideaway booth in a dark café to learn about the problem. They told us all about sea squirts, copepods and lugworm larvae and their importance to the ecological food chain. We were overcome with a sense of stupidity since we barely understood a word they were saying. I was given an armful of zoological and biological books and reams of technical papers and a deadline for an ad.

Twice I returned to my client, beseeching him to pick a hotter subject. "Population control—now there's a zinger subject for a consumer ad," I announced to the nonplussed director. "How in hell can I make magic out of mud?"

But magic was what they wanted, a blockbuster ad on the subject of mudflats that would achieve three impossible goals: (1) The ad had to be technically accurate and yet palatable, indeed fascinating, to the lay reader; (2) it had to be highly persuasive and influential to the movers, the thought leaders, the legislators and have an impact on upcoming legislation; and (3) it had to have such creative excellence as to motivate national publications to give it free public service exposure.

There are countless causes, charities and foundations requesting free space in the pages of *Time, Esquire, Playboy,* the *Chicago Tribune,* the *B'nai Brith Messenger* and even *Turkey World.* When these publications have unsold advertising space, they are delighted to donate it to a public cause. It is often an editorial director who decides who should be the beneficiary of their largesse. Should it be Smokey the Bear or the United Crusade or the Child Abuse Council—or should it be an ad on the subject of mud?

Sitting before my typewriter, sinking ever deeper in the quagmire of mud, I wondered how my boring ad would ever beat the pants off Smokey the Bear. Then it happened. I fell in love, as I have so often. I had a former love affair with Goodyear's triple-tempered tires. My romance with Anthony Swimming Pools lasted for years. I even fell in love once with a gambling casino in Tahoe, Kings Castle, for which I wrote, *New From the 16th Century—Pleasure Kingdom in the Tahoe Woods.*

Now I was in love with lugworm larvae and burning with excitement, ready to write my ad. It would be a tone poem, compelling and compassionate, and I would make the reader feel the anguish of those dying species of life squishing through the mud. And the editors *would* run my ad—free.

Here are the words from that ad:

DON'T MUDDY UP THE GOOGOL*

**Googol: The largest number of things that has a name. Webster defines as the number one followed by a hundred zeroes.*

There are googols of little creatures squiggling and burrowing, flitting and squishing under the mud, through the swamps and over the sandy marshes. Sea squirts, copepods, lugworm larvae and the babies of little fish. Each with a kind of brain, each with the breath of life. But their life is ebbing. And as they start to go—you do, too.

You are standing on the threshold of time in as sacred a place as any in the world. It's where the life of the water and the life of the land converge in biological blur. These are the wetlands—the swamps and the mudflats that sometimes smell like rotten eggs. These are the marshes, clogged with weeds, swarming with bugs, teeming with beautiful life. This is where the moon moves the water in shallow ebbs and floods, where the sun pierces down to the ooze and the nutrients flow in a strange and marvelous way. Nowhere else except here in these sopping grounds is there so much life in so much concentration. But the life is dwindling. And as these lands start to go—you do, too.

These squishy, mushy lands are where most of our fish are born, the fish that feed the fish that feed the fish that fill the sea. These narrow strips of estuarine land are where the birds come to rest and nest and feed; and they are tied inexorably to the life support for the raccoons and the bears and the deer a hundred miles away. And to you.

In California, most of the wetlands are already gone. In Florida, they're going fast. Once there were 127 million acres of interior and coastal wetlands. Now forty percent are gone, the previous specks of life in these lands exchanged for yacht clubs and marinas and industrial growth. As we dredge the bays and fill the marshes and cover the mud with asphalt; as we spray our poisons and scatter our waste and spew oil upon the waters—we destroy forever the great forces of life that began millennia ago.

But now we have gone too far. Because this planet belongs not only to us but to them as well—the umpteen zillion other things that fly in the sky and roam on the land and swim in the sea and burrow beneath our feet.

Now, especially now, if we will only stop to think—perhaps we will think to stop.

SIERRA CLUB

Don't muddy up the googol.*

*Googol: The largest number of things that has a name. Webster defines as the number one followed by a hundred zeroes.

There are googols of little creatures squiggling and burrowing, flitting and squishing under the mud, through the swamps and over the sandy marshes. Sea squirts, copepods, lugworm larvae and the babies of little fish. Each with a kind of a brain, each with the breath of life. But their life is ebbing. And as they start to go—you do, too.

You are standing on the threshold of time in as sacred a place as any in the world. It's where the life of the water and the life of the land converge in biological blur. These are the wetlands—the swamps and the mudflats that sometimes smell like rotten eggs. These are the marshes, clogged with weeds, swarming with bugs, teeming with beautiful life. This is where the moon moves the water in shallow ebbs and floods; where the sun pierces down to the ooze and the nutrients flow in a strange and marvelous way. Nowhere else except here in these sopping grounds is there so much life in so much concentration. But the life is dwindling. And as these lands start to go—you do, too.

These squishy, mushy lands are where most of our fish are born, the fish that feed the fish that feed the fish that fill the sea. These narrow strips of estuarine land are where the birds come to rest and nest and feed; and they are tied inexorably to the life support for the raccoons and the bears and the deer a hundred miles away. And to you.

In California, most of the wetlands are already gone. In Florida, they're going fast. Once there were 127 million acres of interior and coastal wetlands. Now forty per cent are gone, the precious specks of life in these treasured lands exchanged for yacht clubs and marinas and industrial growth. As we dredge the bays and fill the marshes and cover the mud with asphalt; as we spray our poisons and scatter our waste and spew oil upon the waters—we destroy forever the great forces of life that began millennia ago.

But now we have gone too far. Because this planet belongs not only to us but to them as well. To the umpteen zillion other things that fly in the sky and roam on the land and swim in the sea and burrow beneath our feet.

Now, especially now, if we will only stop to think—perhaps we will think to stop.

Sierra Club

The only measure of success for an ad is the results it achieves. The googol ad reputedly garnered more free exposure in the national press than any ad in the history of public service advertising. Since the space was donated instead of purchased, it is impossible to calculate the total media dollar value, but it is surely in the tens of millions. There is hardly a major national magazine which did not run the ad once or more. It appeared in hundreds of newspapers and in some of the most obscure and esoteric trade publications. For more than five years the little ad about mud had been going strong, and I hope it is still very much alive and kicking.

Next time you write an ad or engage an ad to be written or simply read an ad—concern yourself with the concept. Is it a good concept? Is it a strong, persuasive concept? The best concept is the AMAZING, NEW. But if that ingredient simply isn't in the cards—try a little love.

CHAPTER V

CHRIST: WHAT A SPECTACLE HE MADE OF HIMSELF

He took his campaign to the streets. And what a spectacular it was! In the heart of the major markets—Jerusalem, Nazareth, Bethany—he performed with a style of his own. And the crowds roared their approval. His were more than stunts. His was pure magic. He fed the multitudes on five loaves of bread and five little fishes. He whispered to the deaf and at once they would hear. He made blind eyes see. He even awakened the dead. Hard sell it wasn't. Heart sell it was.

This chapter is about spectacles, street demonstrations, parades, drama in the streets and in the stores. Before the printing press and electronic media, all advertising was accomplished in the streets, in the synagogues, in the marketplace.

Can we not learn from the greatest teacher of all that the medium of the streets is still a viable place to promote a good idea? Call them stunts or wild ideas—we, too, can create magic in the streets and in the markets. That was my plan for Folger's Coffee. All I needed was 100 midgets.

For many years, before the Folgers sold out their marvelous family-owned coffee company to Procter & Gamble, I had the pleasure of creating their advertising.

And what smooth sailing it was, because my client was not some numb-nuts product manager with manicured nails but the brothers Folger, Jim and Pete.

I went through a Dr. Frankenstein-like process creating an animated TV character who became famed throughout the western United States as the animated Folger Coffee Bean. It was a precursor to the California Raisin Advisory Board dancing raisin—indeed it was a very similar visage, save the wrinkles. The Folger Coffee Bean was shaped like a bean and had huge Betty Boop eyes, a mouth that wouldn't stop and spindly arms and legs. The Bean appeared in a heavy saturation television campaign for years and uttered such professorial insights as: "Today's subject, Red China. [In those days, it was O.K. to call it that.] Whatever kind of coffee cups you use, plastic, glass, ceramic—or red china—be sure to serve Folger's Coffee, Mountain-grown in the Flavor Zone."

I trust the reader will spare me a critique of that commercial because it relates to a curious promotion for the streets and stores of the Western U.S.

Too few advertising agency people get into this exciting area of communications because there are no commissions and they are simply not comfortable taking off their Giorgio Armani suits and occasionally putting on the clothes of a clown.

The Folger's Coffee Bean campaign had run on TV for a number of years, and it was high time to get that cute little bean right into the grocery stores where he could be even more effective at the point-of-purchase. The plan was not simply to emblazon the little fellow on hanging banners or cardboard, die-cut merchandising displays. I wanted a real live coffee bean to call on the stores.

The promotion was as simple as it was bizarre. The animated Bean would announce on television that he would be calling on grocery stores. Then he would actually appear suddenly and unannounced at the checkout counter. If he found a customer with Folger's Coffee in her cart, the Bean would pay for her entire grocery purchase. Newspaper ads would post the names of the week's winners and public relations would give extra mileage to the promotion. The question was, how do you hold a casting call for a bean? Ah ha! We would employ the services of 100 midgets and place them inside Bean costumes.

The famed Western Costume people in Hollywood were engaged to design a Bean costume to exact specifications. Weeks later and at considerable cost, they came up with a brown fiberglass configuration with huge goo-goo eyes that could be whirled around by swiveling a lever inside. Brown gloves, with little padded hands, were designed to pull tightly up to the shoulders and tiny brown leotards whose feet were designed to look like what you would imagine to be a Bean's feet, completed the illusion.

Now, to find a typical midget to climb into the bean costume so that the idea could be presented to the Folger brothers.

Only a week before the presentation, I glanced out of my 6th-floor office window and to my delight observed, some three blocks away, the perfect midget walking down the street. Actually, I had seen him in our business district before and always admired the confidence and bearing with which he would march down the street as if he were six feet six.

"I found him, I found him! Get that midget!" I screamed to my secretary. She raced to the window and then out the door. Minutes later she returned almost in tears. When made the offer of his lifetime, the little man simply flipped her the bird.

Fortuitously, I located an organization of undersized people. When I phoned, a squeaky voice identified herself as an executive in the organization, and she agreed to visit my office and discuss my plan to engage 100 midgets throughout the West to implement the promotional scheme. She also offered her services for my initial presentation. When she revealed she was three feet short, I hired her on the phone; obviously, her physical beauty did not matter since she would be incarcerated inside the Bean costume. I will not reveal the name of this little lady for reasons that will soon become apparent.

When she walked into my office, I could hardly wait to get her into the Bean costume. I led her to the projection booth off our conference room, where I had stored the costume. Minutes later out walked my real live Bean.

I took a pudgy, upholstered hand and escorted her into the reception room to begin trying her out on the office staff. Somehow the upholstered feet got tangled and she tripped, causing the Bean to do a complete roll-over across the reception room floor, a high-pitched screech emanating from the fiberglass enclosure, startling the hell out of the receptionist.

However, the little lady recovered swiftly from this awkward debut, and after learning that navigating the Bean costume required some skill, she resolutely continued her parade through the offices. There were shrieks of glee from the agency staff. I knew I had a winner on my hands.

The Folger brothers held their periodic sales meetings at the family estate, a multi-million dollar spread in Woodside, California. Attended by some forty wholesale coffee salesmen and Folger executives, this would be the site of the advertising presentation which would feature "the Bean-in-the-Grocery-Store" promotion.

The midget, or "little person," as she preferred to be called, was driven to the Folger mansion by the agency mail boy, who delivered her to a back entrance and set her up in a dressing room. She would be cued at the proper time during my presentation to make her appearance at the podium. My confidence gave way to nervous trepidation, however, when the mail boy informed me that the little lady had put the make on him in the car. Indeed, she had given him evidence that she was perhaps the world's tiniest prostitute and available to provide all variety of new adventures for the man who had tried everything else.

I should mention that the Folger brothers, Jim and Pete, were gentlemen of the most proper moral character. Proprietors of an old and elegant family business, they were ill-disposed to find anything of even the slightest off color amusing.

But just as the show must go on, so must the advertising presentation. The Bean made her entrance, this time without tripping over her feet, and I made my pitch to the sales staff and the Folger management. All went swimmingly until after the meeting and during cocktails, when the Bean reappeared.

I shuddered to imagine what the Bean was saying, but judging from the looks on the salesmen's faces I considered the worst. It was not until I observed the bulbous fiberglass creature chit-chatting with Peter Folger that I realized my brilliant new promotional scheme might be doomed.

With as much grace as could be mustered under the circumstances, I escorted the Bean to her dressing room. She was placed in a taxi and shipped home.

For months thereafter I kept the Bean costume propped on a chair in my office, a lifeless shell, as dead as any of thousands of great advertising campaigns and brilliant promotional schemes that, for one reason or another, never got off the ground. Entombed in advertising agency file cabinets across the land are countless treasures of equal ingenuity, which, deprived of the right timing and adventuresome spirits, and sometimes snafued by one inappropriate, careless, or overenthusiastic gesture will never, ever amount to—beans.

To rally the masses for a noble cause, Christ brought sublime theater right out into the streets. I would follow his lead for a cultural cause with a nobility of its own. It was a crusade to prevent the imminent extinction of the oldest ballet company in the United States and among the finest—the San Francisco Ballet.

What I knew about ballet you could stick in your toe shoe. That's why I was perfect for the assignment, because the idea was to go out into the streets and get the whole community involved, not just the ballet aficionados, grande dame patrons and the sugar-daddy benefactors.

Bill Meyer was a guy with an incessant smile. A ballet board member, he volunteered to head up the fund-raising. He was also president of Swensen's Ice Cream and so persuasive you would melt. When he laid his smile on me and my soft-hearted associate, Jerry Gibbons, we dropped everything and joined his impossible crusade.

Bill thought he could raise a half million dollars in three weeks. If he didn't there would be no more S.F. Ballet because creditors were lining up at the stage door. Grace Costumes wanted their $25,000; Capezio's, which manufactured the delicate shoes, had a bill for nearly $6,000 (one pair of ballet shoes lasts one performance only). The Opera House carpenters wanted their $12,000 for dismantling the symphony shell to make room for the dancers. The bills kept coming in. It was a sad day in August when the ballet board examined the options: (1) perform the *Nutcracker,* pay off some bills, and then go into receivership; (2) keep the ballet school going, but close down the company at once; (3) declare immediate bankruptcy.

The impossibility of Bill's dream to save the ballet was highlighted by the demise of the National Ballet of Washington, which after the most vigorous fund-raising drive was forced to close its doors. With the Hartford Ballet and New York's Harkness Ballet slipping fast, how in heaven did this cocky ice cream vendor think he could save the San Francisco Ballet without pulling off a miracle?

When a letter from the dancers was read at the board meeting, there was hardly a dry eye in the house. The dancers offered to perform free if they had to; they offered to hustle money in the streets—anything to save their precious company. The dancers would, indeed, go out in the streets and confront the people with their crusade.

In ballet circles, the name of the late Lew Christensen inspires awe. Former artistic director of the San Francisco Ballet, he was, during his dancing days, a *danseur noble,* premiering many classic roles with the New York Ballet. He reacted with understandable contempt when I suggested that he bring the whole company to the northern California theme park, Marine World/Africa USA, for a fund-raising presentation of *Beauty and the Beast.* With live chimpanzees yet, and birds of prey and a 500-pound Bengal tiger.

Michael Smuin, Christensen's talented associate at the time, thought it was an amusing idea but, of course, out of the question. Bill Meyer thought it was a smashing idea. When Christensen stomped out of my office with little of the grace for which he is so famed, we all knew the bizarre fund-raising idea was a go.

Jerry Gibbons called Westinghouse television and asked if they would give us a prime time hour on KPIX to televise *Beauty and the Beast* with wild creatures of the jungle performing with the San Francisco Ballet. The answer was yes. Then I called Art Twain, famed for his Levi's jingles. Twenty-four hours later he had a "Fill the Slipper" jingle fully produced, with orchestra, singers, the works. Bill Graham, the rock entrepreneur, kicked in money to pay for a newspaper ad. The radio and TV stations, saying in effect, hell yes, it's a good cause, gave public service time. Everyone I called, everyone Bill called, everyone everyone else called, said yes. The ballet administrators even called Walter Cronkite, and he, too, said yes—and campaigned on network TV to save the S.F. Ballet.

But it was in the streets and outdoor marketplaces where most of the action occurred. The glamorous Lia Belli, then wife of the famed lawyer Melvin Belli, threw a block party. Socialite Pat Montandon threw another. Thousands of revelers filled the streets and filled the dancers' slippers with money. And throughout the city, night and day, thirty-five dancers were on their toes, performing in store windows and on street corners. They even performed at a 49er game; when the scoreboard flashed 49ERS SUPPORT OUR SAN FRANCISCO BALLET, hundreds of football fans reached into their pockets.

Then there was the parade. Was it ever outrageous. City Hall granted the first permit ever allowed for a march of a wild animal parade through downtown San Francisco. Waldo, the talking water buffalo from Marine World, went through the huge plate-glass window of the Bank of Canton, as the photographers clicked away. Members of the San Francisco Ballet Auxiliary hustled contributions as the parade traipsed down Kearny Street and headed for Union Square. In front of I. Magnin's, an elephant volunteered a deposit. The Ballet people in their *Nutcracker* finery danced in the streets.

The spectaculars in the streets brought outpourings of money and love and, because of the wide publicity, letters and contributions from every one of the fifty states. From New York, Leonard Bernstein sent $100. From Montana, Senator Mike Mansfield mailed $50. A little girl in Little Rock sent in a little contribution. People in Europe were heard from, too. But it was San Francisco and the towns around the Bay Area that really came to the rescue. "I'll probably never see you perform," said one small contributor, "but I like to know you're still there." One mysterious local benefactor sent a check for $50,000.

We raised $485,000, and the San Francisco Ballet was saved. I didn't save it, and Bill Meyer didn't save it, nor did the electronic media, with all their power. Who did? The people. It was the people, who left their homes to celebrate in the streets, who lined the thoroughfares for the big parade, who gasped in respectful wonder at the famed ballerinas in shop windows, who gave their nickels and dollars on street corners because they had faith in a beautiful idea.

I remember as a child that marvelous smiling Planters Peanut who bent down to shake my hand. And the pretty girl on roller skates passing out sample packs of Lucky Strikes, with today's knowledge, not a very lucky strike at all. Next time you want to make some noise, news and excitement, maybe you should take to the streets and meet your prospect eye to eye.

There's a funny little man who wears a sandwich board. You can see him most any day on Market and Powell in downtown San Francisco. Those ad men who ignore or pooh-pooh the power of the streets would be well advised to read his sign with its five simple words:

YOU CAN LEARN FROM JESUS

CHAPTER VI

CREATE A MIRACLE NOW

My client Bill Lloyd created what he, his associates and investors regarded as a mini-miracle. It was a curious appliance that had never existed before. It was a first.

Bill had invented the world's first electric douche.

Part marketing man, part medicine man with an engineering talent, Bill had applied the technology of the Water-Pic in creating this innovative hygienic device. Now what to name it? Pussy-Pick? Womb-Broom? We settled on Aqua-Fem.

Aqua Fem would retail for $39.95 and would at first be marketed in the cosmetic sections of better stores. While the Aqua Fem factory worked on getting the bugs out of the apparatus, the marketing and advertising plans went full steam ahead.

My assignment was to position the new product in the consumer mind as an important advance in feminine hygiene and create an insatiable demand for the gadget. But what I knew about douching you could stick in your ear. One hardly goes to the library with the expectation that there is a book called *The History of Douching*.

Should a woman write such an advertising campaign? After all, the traditional ABCs of advertising copywriting state that a product should first be tried out.

But this is not necessarily true. A canny writer and good salesman can vicariously become the consumer, any consumer. For all I know, the famed Jock Itch campaign was created by a woman. I always wondered about that campaign. Like, what is jock itch? Who ever had it? And can there really be a large enough market of people suffering from the dilemma to support such a huge national advertising budget? And who, other than jocks, would wear or associate with jockstraps in the first place? Come to think of it, a woman probably did write that campaign. But back to douching...

In the days when Aqua Fem was to make its big splash, the media was still quite timid about providing space for advertising personal products. So my concern in creating the campaign was not only to persuade the consumer to buy the product but to persuade the media to run the ads. The ads would have to be very tasteful indeed.

As I sat staring at the blank yellow paper in my typewriter, the ludicrousness of my assignment made it increasingly tough to come up with a viable idea. My fingers began typing headlines that my mind would not accept:

**DOUCHE UNTO OTHERS
AS YOU WOULD HAVE OTHERS
DOUCHE UNTO YOU.**

**INTRODUCING
THE IMMACULATE
CONTRAPTION.**

The awful thought struck me: "My God, who would ever *buy* such a device? What kind of persuasion would be necessary to induce a fastidious lady to insert an electrically powered prod into her vagina?"

More headlines raced through my mind. Maybe for a Christmas promotion:

**YES, VAGINA,
THERE IS A SANTA CLAUS.**

I tore the paper form the typewriter. To pull this one off I needed a miracle.

The creative process is not all that mysterious. There are some very simple techniques that can produce marvelous and relevant ideas almost in a flash. Usually, when you get stuck it's because you're *focusing*. The answer is to *unfocus*. I was focusing on words, on headlines.

I pulled back, sat back in my chair and began to explore what I was really selling. I was not selling a vaginal prod that squirted aerated water in eight directions. I was not selling an AMAZING, NEW anything. What I was selling, I decided, was loveliness, cleanliness, beauty, femininity—all those soft and graceful things.

I returned to my word processor, not to write words, but to write a picture. I typed what the picture would be. It would be a woman, pretty but not too pretty. She would be refined, intelligent. The setting would be attractive, tasteful. She would be holding the elongated nozzle and look squarely into the lens of the camera. And she would make a statement—candid, discreet, disarming. I had the picture so clearly pictured in my mind that it was the lady in the picture, not I, who wrote the headline:

**This is exactly what
you think it is.
And isn't it marvelous.**

After the headline, the rest came easy. There would be no mention of the electrical aspects of the device, though I would use the words "modern appliance" to suggest its power source.

The scandalous thought occurred to me that some women would enjoy the gentle massaging action. But, heavens, I didn't dare sell the machine as a sex toy. Still, I was loathe to overlook any segment of the potential market. The language would certainly have to be as pure as my thoughts were prurient. Something like: "It gives you a soft, warm kind of mini-shower. It makes you feel beautifully refreshed."

The photography session was scheduled, the model selected, the props arranged. We were oh so careful about the glint in her eye, the tilt of the nozzle, the composure of her lips. It could be a dynamite photograph, and that was good, but it could also blow up right in our faces. At that photo session, we were very, very careful.

Now please read the copy from the ad. If you are persuaded to purchase the product...I'll tell you later why you can't.

THIS IS EXACTLY WHAT YOU THINK IT IS. AND ISN'T IT MARVELOUS.

Gone are the indignities of the rubber syringe, the hose and nozzle and that horrid thing on the bathroom door that never really was your bag. Say hello to an absolutely marvelous new idea. Aqua Fem.

Aqua Fem is the modern appliance for douching. Lightweight, portable and attractive. You can actually display it on the back of the commode just like a stylish tissue box. It gives you a soft, warm kind of mini-shower. It makes you feel beautifully refreshed. Not just clean, but immaculate. It takes all of 55 seconds. Aqua Fem is so simple one wonders that it was not invented long ago. You simply remove the attractive cover, invert it and fill it with warm tap water. Place the inverted cover on the Aqua Fem base and add your douching preparation. The water is drawn through a retractable tube and out the douching tip. The feather-touch control allows you to regulate both the water flow and its pressure. That's all there is to it.

Many years in research and development, this deceptively simple appliance provides cosmetic and hygienic values never accomplished before. Instead of one forceful jet of water, the Aqua Fem douching tip releases a gentle current of aerated douching solution in eight directions. Aqua Fem insures more effective and thorough cleansing even within the vaginal folds, providing four times the cleansing efficiency in one-third the time.

Incomparably effective by the highest clinical standards, Aqua Fem is the definitive cosmetic appliance for the fastidious woman.

Aqua Fem is for the woman who has just about everything—including an occasional discomfort and maybe a tiny fragrance she'd rather not have.

Aqua Fem is for the very feminine you, the totally womanly you who insists on nothing less than being absolutely civilized.

Available at $39.95 in the cosmetic section of I. Magnin, and other fine department stores.

AQUA FEM

I. Magnin in Los Angeles and San Francisco were the principal opening outlets for Aqua Fem. Large, full-color double-truck ads were scheduled for Sunday supplements in the *Los Angeles Times* and the *San Francisco Chronicle.* Though some of the I. Magnin floor sales staff giggled during their brief sales training demonstration, they soon accepted Aqua Fem as an important new product for which they were prepared to give their all.

And the results? The Monday after the Sunday ad, the Los Angeles store had virtually sold out its large inventory by noon, and the San Francisco store was doing a very profitable business in moving the douches out.

The stores reordered, and Aqua Fem got very busy expanding production, outlets and markets. It seemed that while the ladies were cleaning up, Aqua Fem Incorporated would be cleaning up, too.

Then the complaints started to come in. "Mine leaks." "Mine hurts." "Mine flooded the bathroom." The stores got concerned. The beautiful center aisle displays wound up on the back shelves. Finally, the gadgets went on sale and the huge warehouse inventory was funneled into cut-rate drugstores.

Miracles can come in a flash. But sometimes they turn out to be just a flush in the pan.

The two-year California drought left a lot of people praying for miracles. The drought was the most severe of the century, and California was facing its driest year in recorded history. Grass stopped growing and you could count ribs on cows; entire lakes dried up, their bottoms cracked like the surface of the moon. Many communities rationed water and Californians became very preoccupied with their toilet bowls. "In this land of drought and sun, we never flush for Number One," became the battle cry. The huge agricultural industry was dying on the vine, and businesses such as nurseries and car washes stopped doing business.

During this unpropitious time, one of my clients was Anthony Pools, the world's largest builder of swimming pools. California was its largest market. "If it doesn't rain soon," lamented Bud Weisbrod, Anthony's president, "we'll need a miracle just to keep afloat." The assignment was clear: Produce a miracle now!

A few facts about Anthony will highlight the company's desperation. In the second drought year, Anthony was programmed to build around 6,000 pools throughout the United States for a total gross revenue of some $60 million. Two-fifths of Anthony's business would come from California alone, where $24 million in sales were threatened. In Los Angeles, pool sales were drying up; in northern California they had all but evaporated overnight.

An average pool is filled with about 25,000 gallons of water. A few thousand more gallons are needed to mix with the concrete to build the pool in the first place. The water shortage in northern California's Marin County had become so critical that watering one's lawn with a hose was forbidden and washing one's car was a crime. Marinites kept their shrubs alive with dirty bathwater salvaged from a rare bath which often found two in a tub. Under such circumstances, you can imagine the horror neighbors would feel if an Anthony rig pulled in to build a pool.

And all Bud Weisbrod wanted was a miracle.

We looked for options, but there didn't seem to be any. In some counties, for instance, water was already rationed; there was barely enough to bathe in, much less to swim in. In other areas where water was not actually rationed, anyone caught building a pool could be tarred and feathered by the neighbors. What to do?

The answer came through a combination of inverse logic and free association. The thought process went something like this: We would build a new kind of swimming pool that *didn't use water*. But who would buy such a pool? We'd have to put water in the pool, but whose water and where from? Could we truck the water in from another area? What about evaporation? And how could a new pool owner prove to his neighbors—when everyone was talking about energy conservation—his concern for water conservation? Especially when the state Assembly was preparing legislation to ban all new *heated* pools?

Then Anthony executive Al Strausser volunteered a surprising fact: "Did you know that official Olympic swimming pools are only five feet deep?"

This suggested that the average home pool if it were limited to a depth of five feet, would save 10,000 gallons of water. And you can do anything in a five-foot pool you can do in a ten-foot pool—except maybe a high dive. And imagine the energy that could be saved with 10,000 less gallons of water to heat.

Strausser was a treasure trove of ideas. "Paint the bottom black, and the water will better retain the heat." Jerry Gibbons suggested a pool cover at night to further reduce the energy loss. That miracle for which Bud Weisbrod so yearned was strangely taking shape. Until the end of the drought, Anthony would truck in water; and invent a new pool to boot...one that not only conserved water but saved energy too.

There must be a moment, actually a nanosecond, of magic—when the blood boils hotter and the brain pounds with a special spirit and the metabolism churns with its own secret secretions—that an idea begins to germinate. Then, somehow, within the cerebral folds that idea starts to figure itself out. And suddenly, in a miraculous flash, a few simple words appear from the subconscious: THERE'S A FORD IN YOUR FUTURE, or BETTER BUY BIRDSEYE, or A LITTLE DAB'LL DO YOU, or LET YOUR FINGERS DO THE WALKING, or IT'S THE REAL THING. A few simple words, strung together in a proper order, can have enormous power. Why, they could save a company, secure the jobs of hundreds, protect an investment in millions, and, with the aid of the mass media, even create a kind of miracle.

For Anthony Pools those simple words were:

INTRODUCING THE AMAZING NEW ECOLOGY POOL

Those six words headlined this full-page ad, which appeared in newspapers throughout California.

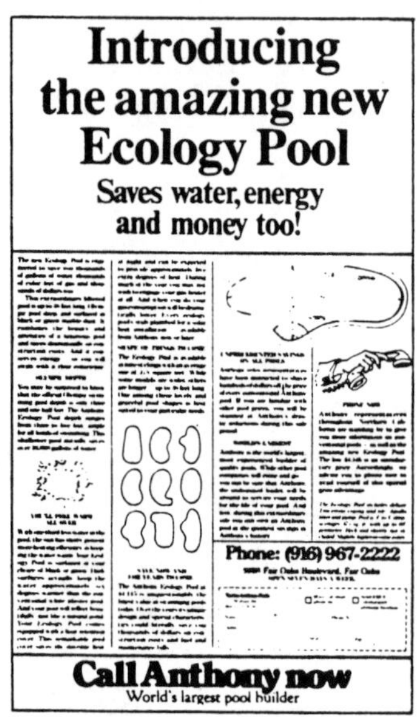

While the drought continued throughout the year, success rained down on Anthony, as the company was flooded with orders for The Amazing Ecology Pool. In the annual report, Anthony's chairman of the board revealed that the year's results "were startling. The number of pools built in the drought-stricken areas exceeded a normal rainfall year by over 13%."

The guy who first sat down and drew a light bulb over somebody's head to symbolize an idea really had the right idea. Because that's how ideas come—in a flash, from out of nowhere. Suddenly, an idea turns on. Where does it come from? How is it generated? What kind of controls can the creative person exercise to turn on an idea at will?

To the professional, these are beginning questions. If you are a professional, you should be concerned with a more advanced question: not simply how to turn on an idea, but—far more difficult—how to *turn on a idea that's absolutely brilliant*. In short, how to *create the miracle.*

The groundwork for producing the miracle marketing or advertising idea is the same as for an ordinary idea. Certainly you learn all about the product that you can. You study competitors' advertising. You search for a unique selling proposition. You get an understanding of the pricing, distribution, marketing background. You determine the importance of finding an idea that is merchandisable at point-of-purchase. You evaluate the temperament of the client. You settle on general marketing objectives. Having digested all that intelligence and cerebrated at some length about demographic groups and media possibilities, you can put your brain at rest. Because from now on, in your search for a brilliant idea, your brain is probably the least important factor.

You've thought about things. Now it's time to *feel* things, to sense them. You've used your brain, now you need to start using your heart, backbone, nerves, glands, guts. Those are the organs that produce ideas of brilliance, the miracle concepts.

You've searched *out* the problem; now it's time to search *in* for the solution. Brilliant ideas don't come from without; they come from within. And the farther out the idea, the farther *in* you must go in your search. To state it another way, in order for you to find the brilliance from within you must ignore the commonplace from without.

About the masses to whom you are expected to communicate: ignore them—especially them. Talk to yourself. And only yourself.

Mass communications? They're a myth. If you sit down and deliberately, scientifically, and methodically attempt to communicate with the masses, you wind up communicating with no one. If you don't belive me, try writing or talking to the masses, that great composite, faceless face out there. What in the world would you say? For years advertising men have been "communicating" with the masses with common-denominator phrases such as "Good morning, good muffin to you." Or, "Gets your whites whiter and your brights brighter." Or, "Fill it to the rim with Brim" *(chuckle, chuckle)*. And so forth.

The art of brilliant communication can only be achieved when you address yourself not to the masses but to a single person. That single person to whom you write your ads should be no one else but you. When you sit down and write an ad, ask yourself: What would reach me? What would sell me? Then proceed to sell yourself. Write to yourself. "Yourself" will, of course, become the Marilyn Reynolds of my dedication, as you mysteriously transmogrify yourself into "everyman" and "everywoman."

Where does that leave all the marketing research that stratifies people into demographics and psychographics, with the expectation that copywriters and art directors will tailor their writing and their pictures accordingly? Where does my technique of "write to yourself" leave all that marketing data? It leaves it out in the cold. Remember now, we're not talking about creating just good ideas. Traditional marketing tools can be very helpful when you're dealing with traditional advertising forms for which there are predictable measures. But we're talking about brilliant ideas.

When you write by yourself, for yourself and to yourself, you write with honesty. And when you write with honesty—disarming honesty—you disarm people. And when people are disarmed, their defenses come down. They are ready to surrender. You can't write that kind of honest, incisive stuff if you write to demographic groups. You can if you write to yourself. Mass communications? Baloney! I'm reluctant to bring out those classic and brilliant Volkswagen ads, which almost revolutionized advertising, for yet another review. But I assure you they made no attempt to talk to the masses, and that's why they reached the masses with such stunning impact. Ideas you can get any time. Brilliant ideas are what we are exploring now. So, copywriter, sit right down and write an ad to yourself.

A very effective technique is to start out with an absurd premise. Let's say you have a fertilizer client. Fertilizer can be odoriferous, unpleasant to touch, and, though often a synthetic or chemical blend, most people think of it as excrement from a cow. Why not start with the absurd premise that fertilizer is beautiful, indeed poetic? It is, you know, because fertilizer is a marvelous fuel that helps food grow and flowers bloom.

Start with an absurd, impossible, outlandish premise. Then find a way to make it work in a relevant way. To illustrate the effective but gentle action of a shaver, Hanly Norrins took a Remington and shaved the fuzz off a peach. Don Miller put a Chevrolet and a beautiful girl on the pinnacle of Castle Rock, 7,200 feet in the clouds. Betty Crocker sold a lot of cake mix because some copywriter started with an absurd premise that led to a brilliant idea for a television commercial: *Betty Crocker cakes are so tender, you can cut them with a feather.* And that's exactly what happened before your eyes on the TV screen.

I recall sitting in my tiny office at Young & Rubicam in New York searching for a television idea to dramatize the strength of Goodyear's new triple-tempered tires. And the absurd, impossible premise struck me. I would take a car equipped with the new tires to the moon, over whose rough, jagged, pocked surface the tires would prove their strength in a tortuous test drive.

The impracticality of getting an automobile to the moon eluded me as I constructed the commercial on the screen of my imaginings. I could hear the theremin wailing strange moon music as some extra-terrestrial camera moved in for a medium shot of the moon. Then the scene would dissolve to the ragged, jagged surface of the moon and the camera would pan to a distant crater. We'd hear a car start up and the roar of an engine, and from behind the crater a car would appear, and then race across the surface of the moon. The camera would be very close on the tires as they took a beating no tires had ever taken before. Perhaps the eerie voice of Ken Nordine would narrate this extraordinary first. And then I woke from my meanderings. What an absurd premise. Or was it?

Of course I couldn't get a car to the moon. Or could I? When you start with an absurd premise, you must try to follow it through to a practical solution. The real moon, I despairingly concluded, was out of the question. But how about an ersatz moon? A few hours of research revealed to me that there was an area in Oregon called Valley of the Moon, whose terrain conformed to everyone's perception of the surface of the real moon. And with craters yet.

It would be the exact commercial I had visualized. The voice-over announcer would simply provide a qualifier. After the dramatic opening moments he would say, "Well, we couldn't get to the real moon. So we went to the next closest thing to it—Valley of the Moon, Oregon."

Once you've come up with a brilliant idea, the kind of an idea for which there is no precedent, an idea that nobody else has ever dealt with before, how in the world do you sell it to your client? If you *are* the client, how do you reconcile such a commitment?

An advertising client should be a solid businessman. Often he is responsible for the expenditure of millions of advertising dollars. He is beholden to his company's board of directors and stockholders and responsible for the company's reputation. How, for instance, could you persuade him to put millions of dollars behind a campaign that calls his company's product a "lemon" when, in fact, his product is a VW automobile? How *did* Bill Bernbach persuade VW? How can you get a client to underwrite a major capital expense for an advertising idea featuring a man with an eyepatch when everyone knows—particularly your client—that it is unacceptable to exploit the infirmed in advertising?

How do you persuade a client to take such a mammoth creative leap? What do you say when your client looks at you, totally underwhelmed and says, "But will it sell?" When you present the innovative Isuzu campaign to your client and he gives you a you've-got-to-be-kidding look, how do you persuade him to spend 30 million dollars on David Leisure, then an unknown actor, who would portray an obnoxious, pushy car salesman on TV to represent your company by lying about your automobile?

The absolutely brilliant idea, the miracle ad, is created out of conviction and passion—and it must be sold the same way. The level-headed, well-meaning account executive representing the agency will never sell such material if he depends upon the fallible tools of research to back him up. Brilliant concepts that produce the miracle sales results deal with the unknown, the unexplored. Research can measure only against known factors. Far-out ideas that stretch the imagination can't be reached by these tiny tools. The advertising profession needs account executives who will stand up for the brilliant idea and fight for it and sell it. Their tools are their own intuitions, rhetoric, courage and brilliance.

If you want simple, everyday results, simple, everyday advertising will achieve them. There is very little calculated risk. But if you want to reach for the stars, reach deep inside yourself and pull out that one idea that shines with a blinding brilliance. Then find an equally brilliant method of taking the blinders off your client, and sell that idea.

If the client wants practical documentation that your bold idea will mean big business for him, show him the case histories of the great classic advertising campaigns and lay your agency on the line. Compromise born from fear is for cowards and failures. The growth agencies in the U.S. are the agencies that are creating brilliant work and then *selling* that brilliant work to their clients.

There is a happy trend in the air as we watch the intuitive advertising campaigns stealing the show. The companies who are growing, not just in tiny increments on the profit graph, but in bold, dramatic leaps, are all too frequently those companies that assert themselves with the kind of advertising that has never been dared before.

How do you come up with an absolutely brilliant idea? You can free-associate; you can start with the "absurd premise"; you can write *not* to the masses but to yourself. And there are other techniques, which perhaps you yourself have come up with. But basic to all techniques is an attitude of freedom.

Out there floating around in the blue are zillions of ideas, areas of communication that have never been explored. Open your senses to a breakthrough. Don't follow a new trend; create it yourself. The consumer has an appetite for bold, innovative ideas. They're happening all around us: on the motion picture screen, in the pages of popular magazines, in the performing arts. Let them happen in advertising, too. Go out and create yourself a miracle!

CHAPTER VII

THERE'S A SIGN IN THE SKY

Outdoor directional postings have been around a long time. Is it stretching it to refer to the Star of Bethlehem, that bright sign in the sky which directed the Three Wise Men on their historic journey? Did not Christ preach in the forums in competition with outdoor advertisements for circuses and gladiatorial events?

Actually, there was outdoor advertising at least three centuries before Christ's birth, documented by a posting on papyrus which offered a reward for an escaped Theban slave. During the second century A.D., a Roman traveler named Pausanias referred to outdoor announcement signs, which were certainly forerunners of today's billboard. When Britain was still controlled by the Celtic barbarians, public notices were part of the honorable culture of barter. Thus, word-of-mouth communication and the town crier notwithstanding, outdoor postings have an ancient and noble history as the first form of advertising.

It is unfortunate that such enlightened cities as Houston, Portland and San Diego, as well as the entire state of Vermont, are legislating against the future existence of the billboard. In the name of aesthetics and the environment—and of course never in the name of elitism—certain people have put to death a species of the history of civilized communication. Moreover, the species is seriously endangered in hundreds of other cities throughout the United States because of the efforts of those who believe, in their self-serving imaginings, that they are providing a community service.

Actually, outdoor advertising *is* a community service. Billboards provide happy, colorful displays amid acres of concrete boredom; lighting for safety at night in cities ridden with crime; directional information, as on the highway, to goods and services; free public service announcements for important medical and social causes—to the tune of $140 million free service space a year.

Those screaming ninnies who clomp through city halls in their comfortable shoes protesting billboards would probably have attacked the posters of Toulouse-Lautrec with the same fervor. Though they may adore a can of Campbell's soup in a painting on a museum wall, they resent it on an outdoor billboard.

Outdoor signs keep us awake on long, boring drives; tell us of events that have arrived in town; decorate our streets at Yuletide; remind us to vote in elections; and show us the way to San Jose.

Outdoor signs—whether billboards, wall posters, transit postings or lighted spectaculars—are, like the paintings you hang in your home, the public pictures we hang in the town.

Of all advertising media, outdoor billboards can be the cheapest—or the most expensive. They can be the easiest to create or the most difficult. They can be the most effective advertising or the least. So, if your city or town continues to support this medium—and if you have a stake in advertising something, anything—this chapter might well pay you back the price of the book plus a bonus in advertising impact worth a few extra thousand dollars, or even hundreds of thousands of dollars.

If you judge advertising media value on the basis of cost per thousand impressions made, then outdoor billboards have to be the best bargain. On the average, $1,000 spent in outdoor space will deliver 925,000 impressions; that same expenditure will deliver about 450,225 impressions on radio, 224,607 impressions on television; 225,000 impressions in newspaper; 200,000 impressions in magazines. Perhaps the most expensive medium is direct mail. But the cost of the stamp alone will buy you 272 impressions on an outdoor billboard.

However, used incorrectly, as it most often is, outdoor advertising can be very expensive indeed. The communicative power of an outdoor billboard depends upon some very simple principles of color, color contrast, type selection, type spacing, type size and graphic content. Few advertising agency art directors have even the vaguest idea of how to design an outdoor board for maximum effectiveness.

An outdoor billboard is like an optometrist's eye chart. The bigger and bolder the letters, the greater the distance from which the board will be read. The greater the distance the board will be read, the more impressions the billboard will make. The more impressions it will make, the lower will be its cost per thousand people reached. When designing an outdoor billboard, a good rule of thumb is: whenever the letters are as big as you think they can be—make them even bigger.

Quite often the art director seated at his stationary computer, staring at his static billboard design, does not understand that he is creating a motion picture. While of course the billboard doesn't move, the viewer does, often a a speed of fifty-five mph or more. The tiny billboard in the distance gets bigger and bigger, almost as if a camera were zooming in on it. And the second the big close-up occurs, the picture flashes off the "screen."

Meanwhile, the driver of the vehicle is listening to the radio, talking to his companion, watching the traffic to protect his life. The art director must engage enormous skills and restraints in order to create a design that will first interrupt the driver's divided attention and then, at a moment's glance, communicate a message.

The seventeenth-century philosopher and mathematician Blaise Pascal once wrote, "I have made this letter rather long, only because I have not had time to make it shorter." If you are creating an outdoor billboard, take the time to find the fewest words (preferably seven or less) to tell your story.

Tony Eglin used to be the ad manager of Hastings, a fourteen-store chain in northern California featuring expensive men's clothing. The elfin Britisher approached me for some counsel on how to improve his multi-media advertising program.

The store was spending nearly a half million dollars each year on large-space newspaper ads and a much smaller budget combining radio and magazines. One glance at his newspaper ads told me he had a hidden treasure that could yield for Hastings a bonus advertising value of over $150,000 a year.

In an upcoming chapter, we will look at methods by which newspaper ads can be cut to half the size, cutting the media cost accordingly, without in the least reducing their impact or readership. By applying such techniques to Hastings's ads, a vast amount of money could be relieved for use in another medium. For a retail clothier, outdoor billboards would be the most unlikely of all media. I recommended outdoor billboards.

While outdoor advertising has the advantage of the lowest cost per thousand impressions, it has the disadvantage of brevity. You do not write a letter home on an outdoor billboard. If you use more than seven or eight words, you start to get into trouble. Moreover, Hastings was principally in the business of selling men's suits and sports coats, which are traditionally displayed on a vertical model. Outdoor billboards are horizontal. Either I would persuade the outdoor billboard companies to stand their boards on end, or I would be restricted to a model lying prone for each outdoor showing. Retailers run three- and four-day sales featuring price-off advertising. Newspapers, published on a daily basis, provide flexibility for the in-and-out sales. Outdoor boards are generally posted and reposted monthly. It became obvious to me why outdoor billboards were not the clothing retailer's best friend. I could find no evidence that billboards had ever been used as a principal medium for selling retail clothing. I felt that if I could just solve some of the baffling problems, we could be off and running with a breakthrough campaign.

Why not simply break all the rules and create a few new ones?

An effective outdoor board should fill all the space with words and picture, the bigger the better. Therefore, I decided my male model in his Cardin suit would be as big on the board as I could get him. And, yes, he would be lying down. To give the board a little spice, however non sequitous, he would always have one shoe off, exposing a nude foot. And because all other outdoor billboards have color, the Hastings billboards would stand out the most because they would simply be black and white. Further, the absence of color would save on art and print production costs, providing even more dollars for the unusual new campaign as well as provide a visual link to the traditional black-and-white newspaper retail ad with which the consumer was so familiar and comfortable. The quick in-and-out, three-day sales could be handled by use of add-on overprints called "snipes."

Having conjured up a $150,000 ad budget from seemingly out of nowhere, Tony Eglin undertook to research just what it would buy in outdoor impressions in his marketing areas. By buying and scheduling the boards with a few weeks' hiatus between postings, he managed to get over $40,000 in bonus exposure. Since the posting companies could not sell the space for two or three weeks only, they would leave the postings up until they were pasted over with the next in the series. Incidentally, the outdoor billboard is the only medium that provides continued, free advertising exposure if the space is not sold when the contract runs out. I know of no newspaper, magazine, or broadcast medium that provides this bonus.

When Tony finally "figgered," as he would say, the omnipresence of exposure which his new dollars would provide, he was ecstatic. "We'll paper the whole bloody city, we will," he crowed, his Oxonian speech deteriorating into Cockney.

And paper the city Hastings would, with an initial outdoor campaign that would find a Hastings billboard at virtually every turn. Not only would this be the largest outdoor showing in the history of retail advertising, it would be the largest outdoor posting ever mounted by any advertiser in northern California's Bay Area. Indeed, according to Combined Communications Corporation, based on the population center, it would become the heaviest concentration of outdoor billboards for a single advertiser in the history of the world. Tony was beside himself, "It's a blimey breakthrough!"

All we needed was a blimey model. Tony arrived in my office with ten pounds of male-model photo composites. We were about to commence a talent search for a male model to be the Hastings Man to rival Selznick's quest for his female lead in *Gone with the Wind*.

Had we tried for the look of a typical Hastings customer, we would come up with an older gentleman, affluent, conservative and probably bulging in the middle. But that wouldn't do at all. Our Hastings Man would not be the typical Hasting customer but rather have the characteristics the typical Hastings customer perceives when he looks at himself in the mirror: sophisticated, youthful but not young, mature but not old, quite nice looking, and devastating to the ladies. We put a label on the look we were looking for: an over-the-hill surfer.

Our search was compounded and confounded by a couple of other problems. Because it was our expectation that the saturation billboard exposure would catapult the Hastings Man into local stardom, he would be in demand for press interviews, talk shows, and other PR and publicity opportunities. Such activities would inevitably probe his personal life. The proper image of the ultimate man's man and lady's heart-throb necessitated that his name *not* be Harry Lipschitz and that, even in San Francisco, he'd be straight.

At last we found our man. Scott MacKenzie. But why did he have to live in New York? And why did he have to be among America's most expensive models? A thousand bucks a shot!

Turn the page and you'll get the picture...

CERRUTI AT
HASTINGS

A few weeks later, having taken San Francisco and the surrounding counties by storm with the inventive black-and-white saturation billboard displays, we asked ourselves, "What do we do for an encore?"

In the theater, an encore is supposed to fulfill an ever-heightened expectation for more excitement. Few advertising campaigns, whether print or broadcast, undertake to heighten interest or excitement in each successive advertisement. Most continuing advertising campaigns, such as Palmolive Liquid Detergent's series, are content merely to reset the stage for the next ad in the series. While the viewer recognizes the continuity of the same general slice-of-life situation, he understands that a new twist and turn has been added, however simplistic, to prevent total ennui from setting in. So he sits and ignores the new banality. The next Madge commercial will be another one like the former, slightly changed, but never an encore.

For Hastings we would have an encore. And should the crowd scream for more, we would come on for a third encore, and then a fourth, and more, more, more, whipping up ever heightened excitement. We would provide outdoor theatre with the knowledge that each new appearance would upstage the last.

San Francisco, the hub of Hastings's market area, where most of the stores are located, is a cosmopolitan, microcosmic, ethnocentric, international melting pot whose population includes the largest concentration of Chinese outside of China; a historic population of Jewish cultural/financial entrepreneurs as invisible as they are powerful; thousands of Italian millionaires; homosexuals with a collective power that determines the fate of virtually every election; and a hot blend of red-necks, dissidents, do-gooders, opportunists, nif-naffies and eccentrics. Plus a sizable population of just plain, conventional folk, grown accustomed to living in a real-life Fellini movie.

I would not recommend that you measure the success of an advertising campaign by its hate mail, but if the idea has sufficient impact, it will surely have its dissenters. I have known corporate scaredy-cats to stop brilliant campaigns in their tracks, ignoring unprecedented new public awareness and sales increases, while focusing on a handful of negative letters.

In one of the early Hastings billboards, we elected to give model MacKenzie a female companion. Knowing we would flatter the Oriental community, we selected a gorgeous Asian girl and managed graphically to squeeze her onto the billboard in such a way as to not upstage our star model, yet still provide enough space to accommodate the headline. As you study the billboard, I hope you will agree that the models are attractively posed, the message clear and the situation pleasantly romantic and noncontroversial. Not so.

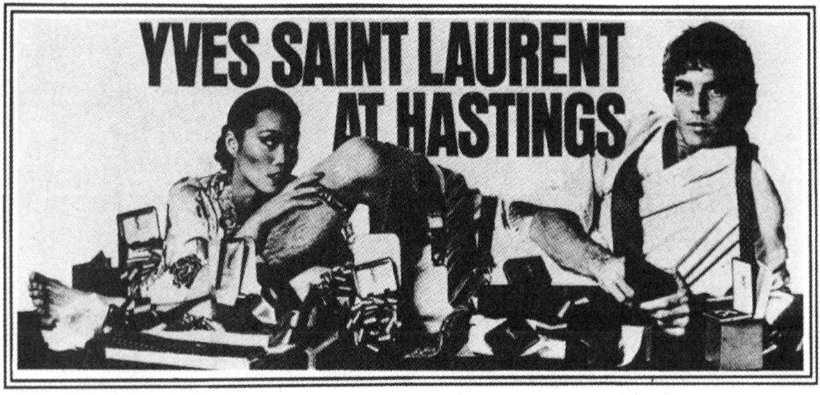

According to the Asian Americans for Community Involvement, the billboard was racist, sexist and offensive. A letter from the AACI to Hastings's ad manager revealed the extent of their consternation:

Mr. Eglin:

Asian Americans for Community Involvement, a civil rights advocacy organization, is deeply offended and insulted by your outrageous attempt to market a product by depicting an Asian woman at the feet of a white male.

The billboard is both racist and sexist and serves only to perpetuate stereotypes of Asian women. This warped and demeaning image in your advertising deserves immediate removal.

We trust your integrity that you will eradicate this distorted imagery and replace it with something more positive. In the future we certainly expect you to be more sensitive towards Asian woman.

Sincerely,
Mary Chan Seid
Chairperson
Public Affairs/Media Committee

Hours after the letter arrived, Tony received a phone call from the organization, demanding that he give them an audience to air the full extent of their grievances. Later, five militants stomped into his office in nearly perfect racial balance: A Chinese lady, a Japanese lady, a black lady and two Caucasians.

Properly British, Tony listened with grave patience to their protestations about white supremacy, sexism and Asian prejudice. He assured the ladies that Hastings had no intention of exploiting Asian women and volunteered that of all the Hastings billboards created to date the one that offended *them* was his wife's favorite. Then, standing from behind his desk as if to signal the close of the meeting, he stated, "Not only is my wife female—she also happens to be Japanese."

He ushered them to the door and thanked them for their social consciousness.

Enzo Belli, the slender, elegant clothier who was Hastings's president and who was concerned about upsetting Hart, Shaffner & Marx, Hastings's corporate parent company, stated to me, "You've offended the entire Asian population. Who do you intend to offend next?"

The next community protest came from an organization that purportedly represented some 100,000 gays in San Francisco. The objection stemmed from a billboard that displayed MacKenzie in shorts.

The billboard had become the talk of the town, so much so that writer Jerry Carroll decided to do a major story on the model in the *San Francisco Chronicle*. In the interview, MacKenzie lamented his relationship with his father. "My father hated me. He used to call me a faggot model. I just sent my paychecks stubs home for a year and he finally shut up."

The gay community registered their feelings with non-stop phone complaints all week. Then came the letter to Hastings's president from the Alice B. Toklas Democratic Club:

Dear Mr. President:

The Alice Toklas Democratic Club is the largest Democratic Club in Northern California, and over 95% of its members are gay. We have a very active organization, taking pride in our fine rapport with local and state politicians, elected legislators and judges. Our primary goals are to further the principles of the Democratic Party and to defend the rights, freedom and dignity of gay people.

A few weeks ago your star model was interviewed in the Chronicle/Examiner. (If you did not see the interview, I urge you to ask your secretary for it.) While it is true that he did not write the feature, it is a fact that in insisting on his heterosexuality he made snide innuendos concerning gays. If he had thought about it for a while, he might have realized that his sexuality was not on the line and did not have to be defended one way or another. In so far as clothing is concerned there is a large choice, and there is no reason for gays to spend their money on unfriendly territory.

Your model's remarks perhaps did more damage to your reputation than all of your admittedly successful advertisements with him on display. Homophobia is reprehensible, as is any kind of bigotry, and it is certainly absurd for your company to be associated with it in any fashion, given the fact that there are over 100,000 gay men in the city of San Francisco alone.

Please show this letter to your model. Also, we hope that you find some way to demonstrate your good feelings towards the gay population.

Sincerely yours,
Roger Silver
Corresponding Secretary

Mr. Belli scribbled on the Toklas letter, "I don't think this deserves an answer." He reminded me that the last billboard had lost him his Chinese customers; the current billboard was losing him his gay customers. "Who do we offend next?" he asked. But his concern surely was tempered by the sales and profit graph in his office, which showed unprecedented increases since the introduction of the innovative campaign.

A concept was needed to promote the August sale. I knew that if I were sufficiently creative I could offend the rest of the city with this one. The parameters within which the boards were designed continued to be very narrow. The model would pose in a horizontal position to accommodate the shape of the medium, and the new billboard would upstage its predecessor with a hot, new surprise.

Because any kind of clutter on an outdoor board will reduce its readability, I chose to stick with a simple silhouette. I thought of all those shapes that could logically be contained within the area of a billboard. Somehow a hot dog bun kept reappearing in my imaginings. Suppose model MacKenzie were placed inside an enormous hot dog bun? Graphically that would be a stopper. But what on earth would the headline say that would make the bizarre picture relevant to the August sale? Considering that I had given myself a restriction of only seven headline words and that three of them would have to be (1) HASTINGS, (2) AUGUST, (3) SALE, I was left with only four additional words. It was a creative algebraic equation, the X factor yet to be figured out. But since all the other good elements were there, I decided I would simply work at the problem until the solution was found.

And finally the solution appeared:

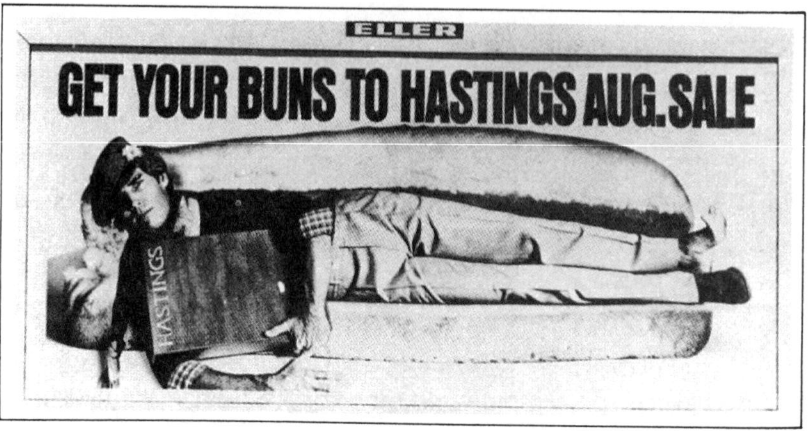

Who did we offend with this one? An editorial in the Glen Park neighborhood newspaper reproduced the buns board and urged readers to phone Hastings at once to protest the tasteless, shameful advertising. Whereas previous billboards had offended only a community faction, the buns board succeeded in offending an entire community. The result was we withdrew all buns boards from Glen Park. But in retaliation, we also canceled all future billboards in the area, effectively denying Glen Park any more titillation.

You are perhaps familiar with the name Dianne Feinstein, formerly president of the San Francisco Board of Supervisors, who assumed the office of mayor to fill out the term of George Moscone, assassinated in his city hall office by one of her former fellow supervisors. Later Mrs. Feinstein won on her own a city-wide election to the office that she assumed with such dignity in the aftermath of the murder. Thereafter, she became a viable contender as a Vice Presidential candidate, the California governor and of course the Senator from California.

For a decade before she became San Francisco's first elected woman mayor, Feinstein was front-page news. She became celebrated during two previous ill-fated election attempts for the office of mayor and was a favorite target of columnists, who nicknamed her "Miss Goody Two-Shoes" and delighted in making bitchy references to her wardrobe, which seemed to feature tweedy suits and silk blouses with large floppy bows.

While Mrs. Feinstein's wardrobe was in fact classic couturier fashion, the "famed" Los Angeles designer, Mr. Blackwell, whose name appears to surface only once a year to designate America's worst-dressed women, honored Mayor Feinstein by placing her just below Bo Derek on his annual listing.

All this may seem irrelevant to Hastings billboards, but patience, please. While Hastings is principally an emporium of fine menswear, a number of their stores include departments of fine clothing for women. I suggested to the management that it consider a billboard reminding the community that Hastings featured women's clothing, too.

I recalled Mrs. Feinstein's public crusades against outdoor billboards and the vigorous defensive crusade waged with media money which helped defeat a Feinstein-supported ban-the-billboards proposition on a citywide ballot. Would it not be amusing to have a Feinstein look-alike sprawled across the outdoor billboards? Amusing? It would be riotous! Feinstein's distinctive coiffure could be easily duplicated, and her trademark, classic school-marm suit and bowed silk blouse were very much in the genre of Hastings's women's fashions. We would simply find a model with her boney cheeks and cheeky smile and there would be no mistaking the visage.

Lest any local be so thick as to miss the joke, Tony Eglin provided a verbal clue for the headline. He studied the name Feinstein. Certainly we would never dare print the proper noun on the billboard. How would we? How could we?

Feinstein. What's in a name? Plenty:

FEINSTEIN
FINESTYLE

Suppose, just suppose, that bad type spacing connected the word FINE with the word STYLE. At a glance (and who gives more than that to a billboard?) the identity of the model would be confirmed. Our final billboard headline read:

FINESTYLE FOR WOMEN TOO.
HASTINGS.

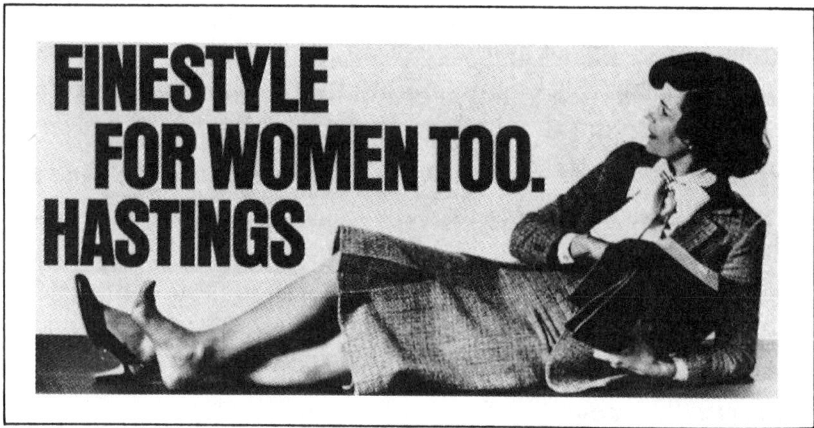

I shuddered with delight at the waves of happy hysteria that this billboard would provoke. The attendant press and television publicity would have a dollar value way in excess of the cost of the billboard medium showing the FINESTYLE advertisement.

Doubtless, the mayor would be confronted by television newspeople for her reaction to the spoof, and I expected the gracious, witty lady would respond with a lighthearted sense of humor—just as she did when interviewed about her selection for Mr. Blackwell's list. "I think I'm flattered," she had said. "After all, I'm in the company of Bo Derek, and she's no slouch."

We planned public relations opportunities to give the press every chance to report on the billboard event. We would feed the press new ideas for stories regularly throughout the duration of the posting. One such PR idea would be the eventual disclosure of the identity of the Feinstein look-alike model, perhaps a short television news interview with the mayor and her look-alike impersonator. I should mention that I lost my battle with Hastings president Belli to have the Feinstein look-alike turn out to be a guy in drag. My God, what a blast that could have been!

The Feinstein billboard would surely infuriate a few, and Hastings was quite prepared for the letters of protest. No doubt many of the boards accessible to pedestrians would be graffitoized, adorning our lady mayor with the usual mustache and monocle and, we hoped, nothing more adventuresome. The Scott MacKenzie billboards had been a favorite of graffiti artists, who concentrated their scribblings in the area of the crotch. One billboard at a busy urban intersection suddenly debuted with an enormous, three-dimensional dork, obviously the handiwork of a skilled sculptor content to revel in anonymous fame. While Hastings would never officially encourage or sanction such hanky-panky, there is no doubt that the graffiti added to the impact of the billboard showings.

Two days before the massive FINESTYLE billboards were scheduled for posting, I decided it would be appropriate to prepare Her Honor for the event. After all, she might be besieged by the press, and I felt it fair that she know in advance what it was all about. I had a miniature of the billboard attractively framed and scrawled on the mat, "Dear Dianne—Thank you for inspiring the most beautiful billboard in town. Bob Pritikin." In the accompanying letter delivered to the mayor that day, I wrote, "I trust your marvelous sense of humor will prevail in the ensuing days when the billboards go up in San Francisco. The people at Hastings look forward to your happy reaction to this light-hearted billboard and hope you understand that any similarity to actual persons is based on affection and respect."

That evening, although I was not expecting a visitor, my doorbell rang. Nor was I expecting the letter, hand-delivered by a courier, from the mayor's attorney. Mayor Feinstein was not amused. The letter referred to State Code 3344, which prohibited the use of "someone's likeness" without prior consent. In the most threatening tone, the letter advised that the billboards be scrapped or else. Also named in the complaint were the president of Hastings and Eller Outdoor Advertising Company of California.

San Francisco's widely read columnist Herb Caen had already been supplied a photograph of the billboard and, as expected, the following day he featured the item in his column. Now the entire city would be hanging on tenterhooks awaiting the posting of the billboards. What to do? What to do?

We reviewed the many options: (1) *Scrap the campaign*. But Hastings had already committed to a huge showing, and there was no other billboard to post. (2) *Run it anyway*. We could take our chances on incurring the wrath of the mayor and losing in an expensive lawsuit. (3) *Run the billboard, but chop off the head*. This procedure would invite the press to headline their stories, THE BILLBOARD DIANNE BANNED. And somehow the press *would* get a photo of the billboard to reproduce. (4) *Censor the eyes*. Hastings legal counsel advised that a diagonal strip across the eyes would get them off the legal hook. But the mayor would look very bad indeed. (5) *Get Feinstein to change her mind*.

Option (5) was the most attractive. We delayed the posting and I confronted Feinstein's closest friends. When they saw the photo of the billboard they howled with glee. The popular state assemblyman Willie Brown, later to become San Francisco's mayor, looked up from the photo and asked incredulously, "Is it really her?" After meeting with a half dozen of the mayor's friends and advisors, I saw a glimmer of hope. They would try to change her mind.

One factor, I felt, should have been particularly persuasive to the mayor. If she persisted in opposing the billboard she would have effectively put look-alike model Grace Wright out of work permanently in the Bay Area. Miss Wright just happened to look like the mayor. I explained to Feinstein's friends that the billboard photograph was not retouched and that the model was not wearing a wig. Surely the mayor would not wish to invoke her authority so as to ruin the career of a professional model. After all, if Miss Wright could not be allowed to appear on a Hastings billboard, in what advertising medium *could* she appear?

After a week of stalemate, the mayor, in a radio interview, agreed to let the billboards go up. Later we learned through the grapevine the reason for her earlier resistance. Apparently, some of her aides, familiar with model Scott MacKenzie and his sometimes half-clad billboard poses for Hastings, had imagined there might be follow-up FINESTYLE billboards, in which the mayor's clothing would be removed step by step until finally she would be displayed in her underwear for all the world to see. Actually, it was a rather marvelous idea, but I assure you it never crossed my mind.

When the billboards finally hit the streets it was like the opening of a long-awaited show. The boards literally stopped traffic, as San Franciscans, inured even to the most bizarre sights, hung from their car windows and laughed out loud.

The story of the billboard Dianne almost banned reverberated through the press of San Francisco, in hundreds of U.S. papers, and throughout the world. Paul Harvey chuckled through the item on the national news. Herb Caen, vacationing in Switzerland, reported back that the story made the *International Herald Tribune.*

Mayor Feinstein has, on occasion, supped at the White House. I think she likes that place. I hope in years to come, should she decide to throw her bow into the national ring, she will give me just a smidgen of credit for getting her known in Conshohocken, Pennsylvania.

During the year and a half that Hastings experimented with this unlikely medium, sales went up incrementally on a monthly basis, all the while the men's clothing industry in the Bay Area was either static or in a state of decline. After eighteen months of billboards, supported with money borrowed from their newspaper budget, Hastings estimated a probable net increase of some 30 percent in gross sales—without any additional advertising costs.

While I have confined my discussion on outdoor advertising to a single client case history, I trust you will explore the medium more on your own. For sheer spectacularity, you might want to study the overpowering painted bulletins that line Sunset Boulevard in Los Angeles, created principally for the egos of recording artists. Nowhere in the world are painted outdoor signs more dazzling than those on the famous Sunset Strip.

As you drive about, search out from the many those few boards which achieve the highest level of graphic excellence and skillfully meet the criteria of producing powerful, instantaneous communication. One of the most powerful billboards ever created, a work of art unto itself, was done by Foote, Cone & Belding for Sunkist Growers. It features an enormous orange, sparking with drops of dew and stamped with the famous SUNKIST brand name. The six monosyllables tell all that needs be said: YOU HAVE OUR WORD ON IT. And remember that your audience may be racing by at fifty-five mph, with but a second or two to glean your message. But if your message is bold and bright and marvelous, it will be remembered all the way to the showroom floor, the ticket cage or the grocery store shelf.

If you are reading this book simply to be amused and think you have no practical application for your new knowledge of mass communications, think again about outdoor billboards. An acquaintance of mine with the curious name of Edwin Heaven was looking for a job as an advertising copywriter. Rather than produce a résumé and traipse around to agencies, he simply purchased a month's showing on a single outdoor board which proclaimed in the biggest, boldest letters:
EDWIN HEAVEN WRITES LIKE HELL.

Yes, Edwin got a very good job. The power of personalized outdoor advertising is further testified to by a New Yorker who posted a few showings of his rather plain face and announced he was looking for a wife. More than 8,000 responses followed. Admittedly, his few postings caused a flurry of news reportage—but, as we have stated, isn't that what a hot ad idea is all about?

In most metropolitan centers, you can go out and purchase for a few hundred dollars a single outdoor showing for a month. Think of all the things you'd like to get off your chest. Well, don't just sit there; go to the phone and call one of your local outdoor billboard companies. They'll be happy to take your money, and you will be reassured that your message will be reaching an average of 1,000 people for less than 60 cents. Quite a bargain considering there are some fancy magazines where the cost of reaching a thousand people with an ad is over $60.

A single Christmas card, including stamp, can easily cost you more than 60 cents. Next Christmas why not consider posting your own mammoth Christmas card outdoors, where that same 60 cents will reach 1,000 of your friends and neighbors?

What a nice way to celebrate the birth of Christ. The Savior would certainly approve. He was a very practical and, one could assume, sublimely frugal man.

CHAPTER VIII

SEEK AND YE SHALL FIND: FREE ADVERTISING

o ye into all the world," Jesus said, "and preach the gospel to the whole creation."

"To the *whole* creation?" observed Bruce Barton in his 1924 best seller, *The Man Nobody Knows*. Why, the man was penniless; without an organization, save a handful of uneducated men, one of whom had already deserted to the enemy. And yet, he had the confidence, the temerity, the inspiration that he could indeed deliver his message to the whole creation.

Public relations can be thought of as free advertising. But it's different from most advertising because most advertising is not news. Public relations deals with that which is new or news.

A good PR person can find news in everything. A brilliant PR person will actually create news. Of course Christ was such a talent. Bruce Barton thought up these headlines, which would have looked great in the *Jerusalem Gazette:*

**JESUS INVADES SYNAGOGUE,
KICKS OUT MONEY CHANGERS**

JESUS MAKES BLIND MAN SEE

**JESUS OF NAZARETH
CLAIMS RIGHT TO FORGIVE SINS**

If your product is sufficiently unique, the news media will "advertise" it for you, absolutely free. And a news story has infinitely more credibility than does a paid ad. So not only is such "advertising" free but it is more effective. You may wish to engage a PR firm or a PR person and pay a modest fee for the possibility of an immense media splash.

A number of years back I was engaged in a real estate negotiation where escrow and timing considerations necessitated that I purchase property at once. After a frenzy of quick decisions, I wound up the owner of a great, sprawling rooming house. When the realtor delivered my title papers, I knew I must have been bereft of my senses. Or was there some secret inspiration churning deep inside me which had not yet revealed itself?

After a few weeks of presiding over the massive Queen Anne Victorian white elephant, with its ragamuffin occupants, I decided to sell it. But to whom would I sell it? To a single buyer? No, I would sell it to "all creation."

I would sell this strange, haunting edifice to millions as the world's most unique hotel. I would create a hotel so unusual, so innovative, so revolutionary as to command the attention of the world press; and any guest who would occupy its rooms would help spread the word.

There are different degrees of impact. If a movie impresses you, you may tell two friends; if it thrills you, you may tell four friends; if it overwhelms you you may tell six friends. But if it overwhelms you *and* devastates you, you may tell everyone you encounter. You will then have become a walking advertisement, for which the producers of the movie have not paid a cent.

I decided I would turn the ramshackle flophouse into an event designed to overwhelm and devastate. Accordingly, I would not have to pay to advertise it. The visitors and guests would advertise it for me, as would the news media.

I have advised a number of my advertising clients not to advertise at all. You can appreciate why most advertising agencies would be loath to make such a recommendation to their clients. While most large agencies maintain public relations departments, the service is provided on a fee basis as an adjunct to the advertising; it is rarely, if ever, recommended as a replacement to advertising.

One day I received a phone call from my friend, writer Gwen Davis, who asked if I would throw a party for her in my home to help launch her new book, *The Aristocrats*. She informed me that luminaries of the likes of Dustin Hoffman would be in attendance. I told her that I would be glad to host the party but that I wanted to hold it in my hotel, not in my home. I would cross-merchandise the introduction of her new book with the introduction of my new hotel. It would be a double-whammy production, a wild and wondrous celebration with sufficient newsworthiness to attract the press in big numbers.

The main drawback was that the party would occur in less than a month and there was no hotel, only an old, floppy rooming house. Obviously, I would have to move very quickly indeed.

New product development and introduction is usually a long, tedious, and costly affair. Cautious corporate executives will go to any expense to avoid making a mistake. By moving more quickly, with the knowledge that small mistakes could occur, they could ultimately save money and interminable weeks of indecision. And they would enjoy the advantage of applying to the problem-solving process their considered judgment and intuitions, which are often sharper tools than conventional research, which leads to compromise and conciliation.

I elected to create my hotel in a dervish-like whirl of hot decisions, all my own. My plan allowed for the certainty of mistakes, but my hotel would exist as a hot attraction in three weeks, not three years.

I gave the roomers notice. Of the nineteen guest rooms, I recognized that I could vacate only seven in time for the opening. So be it. I named the new hotel The Mansion Hotel.

The Mansion would be a first for San Francisco. Why not a first of its kind in the world? It would be an adult, Victorian Disneyland. It would abound with authentic Victorian furnishings and Victorian memorabilia. I would engage three teams of muralists to emblazon the walls with murals depicting turn-of-the-century life. Each guest room would be dedicated to a historic San Francisco figure, a bronze plaque on the door, a mural celebrating his life on the walls. There would be brass beds with thick goosedown Victorian quilts, lace curtains and the guest amenities would include a Victorian silk rose on every pillow.

The public rooms would glitter with crystal and there would be a staff outfitted in weskits, top hats and silk, bustled gowns. They would offer guests and visitors coffee, wine or sherry at no charge.

And there would be so much more: fresh flowers in every room, the music of Bach wafting through the hallways, breakfast served in bed, rose petals sprinkled in the guests' baths and at every turn there would be another surprise.

I would create a legend from a former occupant. Her name would be Claudia, the legendary hauntress of The Mansion. She would perform concerts in the music room. A Victorian wheelchair would be moved to a piano keyboard. Over the back of the chair would be draped the tattered remains of her Victorian gown, the very gown she wore when performing for her friends and family. Timidly, the guests would address the empty wheelchair and request that she play. They would ask for Mozart's Concerto in C Major or Chopin's Polonaise or even the works of Scott Joplin or John Philip Sousa. Whatever the request, the invisible fingers of Claudia would play at once, instantaneously, almost before the thought left the guest's mind to be enunciated in words.

The works of Baniamino Bufano, among the most important sculptors of the twentieth century, who spent his most productive years in San Francisco, would be displayed in the gardens and galleries of The Mansion. I would contact the Bufano Society of the Arts and offer The Mansion as the perfect setting for displaying the monumental bronze *Saint Francis of Assisi,* and the towering, 20-foot *Johann Sebastian Bach* and the countless Bufano treasures sequestered in storage for lack of a suitable public setting for protection and display.

Yes, the Mansion hotel would be an event, an opportunity to apply all that I had learned about new product development, merchandising, promotion and public relations. It would be a sublime opportunity to be my very own client, to take all of my own advice, the kind of dramatic recommendations I had given so many times to clients too timid to act upon them and to advertising agency heads too terrified to even consider them.

But how could this indulgence ever pay off? Were I to propose such a frivolous scheme to the corporate heads of, say, Hyatt or Sheraton, whatever would they think?

There is a tendency in corporate circles to think in terms of bigness. The bigger the more profitable. The entrepreneur should remind himself that a company grossing $100 million can show a year-end profit of one dollar, while another company grossing a half million can show a year-end profit of $300,000.

I calculated the profit potential of my tiny nineteen-room hotel based on 100 percent occupancy. I hypothesized that if the hotel were sufficiently unique as to command saturation news coverage, and that if that news coverage could be restimulated time and again, and if the guests experiences were of such impact as to generate inordinate repeat visits and referrals, why, then, could I not reasonably expect to fill a mere nineteen guest rooms 365 days of the year?

If my rates were competitive, averaging $140 per night, full occupancy would deliver a gross income of $970,900. Add to that additional income from food and beverage services, banquets, weddings and miscellaneous income opportunities, and the place could generate up to $2,000,000 a year. Deducting the overhead of a small staff and operating expenses, the funky rooming house, restored with charm and drama, could become a little money machine.

I had three weeks to pull it off. An antique resource in San Francisco proved to be a treasure trove—four stories of antique funk, junk and memorabilia. I raced through the dusty showrooms making my selections faster than the proprietor could affix his "sold" signs. "I'll take one of those, two of those and that thing over there!" My selections were based on a combination of two factors: low cost and high theater. I was not simply outfitting a hotel; I was creating a theater set, and the higher the drama, the more extensive would be the PR activity and news exposure—

and not the least important, a memorable adventure for the overnight guests, those walking, talking free advertisements so often forgotten as an advertising medium unto themselves.

In moved the furnishings, truckloads every day. The decisions of what went where were made on the spot—no floor plans, no renderings, no fancy decorators with their color swatches and touchy tempers. No nonsense in this job; I was in a hurry.

What a joy it was watching the murals emerge from the walls, costuming the staff, setting the stage for opening night. The party guests would be inundated with pleasures and stunned with surprises. His Holiness Saint Keshavadas, a famed Indian guru, would bless The Mansion in an exotic ceremony. Tammy de Treaux, the world's smallest person, two feet, six inches tall, would serve hors d'oeuvres.

Two thousand invitations went out in the mail to all the social, cultural and political leaders of San Francisco, and most important, to the news media. The invitations stated, "You are invited to a murder in The Mansion." The homicidal hilarity would feature a couple in Victorian clothing engaged in an amorous moment at the head of the grand staircase. The cuckolded husband would appear and shoot the lover dead. The romantic interloper would come crashing down the stairs and expire in a pool of ersatz blood on the floor of the grand foyer. All this and more, more, more. The press release, of course, highlighted the marvelous opportunity for photos.

Dustin Hoffman did not appear, but the who's who and what's what of San Francisco did. And the press and the television cameras were everywhere. Many were so intrigued that they asked to return after the opening night party so that they might do in-depth features on the unusual new hotel. While Gwen Davis and her new book were my springboard PR device (and she enjoyed extensive publicity from the event), it was the new hotel that got the saturation press coverage.

In the days and weeks that followed, the local and national news media presented my little hotel to the whole world. *San Francisco Magazine* and *San Francisco Business* stopped their presses and altered their production to accommodate feature stories on The Mansion. Every major San Francisco television station provided coverage—not just mentions, but mini-documentaries on San Francisco's hot new hostelry. Jerry Hulse, travel editor of the *Los Angeles Times,* wrote an extensive Sunday feature, and his widely read column was syndicated to some 350 newspapers around the U.S. and the world. A front-page feature in the national *Wall Street Journal* generated at least a thousand reservations. *Newsweek*'s television division filmed a report on The Mansion, providing more TV exposure syndicated around the country. "You jump back a century, slow down a bit, and breathe an atmosphere of forgotten elegance," stated the *Christian Science Monitor* in a lengthy feature. *Vogue* magazine published a photo of The Mansion's grand foyer, and dozens of radio stations throughout the country phoned me for on-the-air interviews.

After six months of nonstop news and feature coverage, I assessed the dollar value of the time and space The Mansion was given, free of charge, by the print and broadcast news media: over $5 million. That's what the print space and air time would have cost were it purchased as advertising.

Some of my advertising peers are aghast that I, whose professional career has been advertising, have spent nary a nickel to *advertise* the hotel. It is now a flourishing and profitable hostelry, so well booked that it turns down more reservations than it is able to accept. Its guests and visitors have included such celebrities as Robin Williams, Barbra Streisand, Joan Baez, Eddie Fisher and the late André Sakharov. And notwithstanding obligatory listings in travel/trade directories, no monies have been allocated to consumer advertising. The public relations techniques that lifted this unknown "product" into national and international prominence can work equally well for any product or service—provided that product or service is unique and very special.

Suppose you were to open a hot dog stand. What would you do to make it so special, so unique as to command the attention of the world press? During the forties, a little hot dog stand opened on La Cienaga Boulevard in Los Angeles. But what a hot dog stand it was! It was architecturally designed as an enormous hot dog, later to become a kitsch culture treasure. And what an opening it had—searchlights, limousines, movie stars, the works. The non-stop press coverage that followed put that tiny hot dog stand on the world map.

But what do you do when the hoopla starts to fade, when that which was new grows old? Simply *create* more news. After The Mansion's first eighteen months, it was time to own the media once again, and this time I also had my eye on heavy national exposure. I set aside a budget of $1,000, with the expectation that it would translate into the equivalent of a few hundred thousand dollars in free editorial space and air time.

I volunteered The Mansion to San Francisco's registrar of voters as a polling place. Then I purchased 100 American flags; commissioned a large banner to be made that bore the legend CAST YOUR FATE ★ VOTE HERE NOV. 7; ordered 200 red, white and blue doughnuts; and rented an Uncle Sam costume.

The press release was headlined AMERICA'S MOST POSH POLLING PLACE. It described my respect for the voter and concern for the electorate, which traditionally must cast its votes in someone's smelly garage or basement. The voters in The Mansion precinct would be greeted by Uncle Sam in a phantasmagoric setting of flags and bunting. They would be served coffee from silver urns and cast their votes under crystal chandeliers; and while they waited their turn to vote they would be entertained by the ghost of John Philip Sousa, whose invisible fingers would perform any Sousa march on the magic piano keyboard.

I surmised on election day that the news media would be hungry for stories of human interest, particularly if there were interesting photographic opportunities. You can certainly imagine that the TV anchors would be anxious for filler materials to help them sustain interest during their long hours on camera reporting the returns.

An army of press and television news people came to cover the planned-for-media event. The item was carried nationwide on CBS Network News (put a dollar value on that), and United Press International and Associated Press put the story and picture on the wire to thousands of newspapers. The *San Francisco Examiner* ran a large photo of the flag-bedecked Mansion hotel on its front page, and the same photo feature reached millions more in the pages of the *Santa Maria* (California) *Time,* the *Detroit Free Press,* the *Fort Collins Coloradian,* the *Hays* (Kansas) *Daily News,* the *Chicago Tribune* and countless other newspapers. Cost for that national saturation campaign: under $1,000.

If you're a client, keep the phenomenon of public relations in mind next time your advertising agency suggests to you an advertising budget of $500,000. Maybe there is a free campaign out there. Well, you may have to provide a modest stipend for a P.R. service.

The following year on election day I pulled out all the patriotic props again and invited the press to come see. Damned if they didn't bite again! And that time because I owned my own flags, my overhead was cut to one Uncle Sam costume rental and five dozen red, white and blue doughnuts.

As Gertrude Stein didn't say, "PR begets PR begets PR begets PR." While I don't have much faith in "mentions" (a feature story is so much nicer), occasionally a mention will be observed by a writer or reporter who will find in the snippet some potential for a larger story, perhaps even a feature. When the feature is released, it could then elicit yet another feature in yet another publication. News people often look for feature news opportunities simply by reading between the lines in the news. So a mere mention, while by itself may not contribute much impact, can inspire a tidal wave of publicity. Of course, sometimes a PR stunt can be a crap shoot. As the PR flacks often say: "Advertising you pay for; PR you pray for."

It has been noted that advertising is among the most stressful occupations. Over the years, my relief from the incessant pressure of creating advertising ideas within inflexible deadlines has been to create music. At first I performed only for my private pleasure, to relax the stress of the day. The instrument of my choice was an ordinary carpenter's saw.

Eventually I achieved a modicum of proficiency, sufficient to give me the confidence to perform for friends and acquaintances. Little did I realize in those beginning days that I was later to become America's Foremost Concert Sawist, a billing I immodestly gave myself, but who would dare to challenge it?

After a guest appearance on a local television show where, outfitted in formal tails, I performed "Moonlight Sawnata" with a full baroque orchestral accompaniment, I was approached by record promoters who felt an album featuring my curious talent might have some commercial potential.

Public relations, as we have explored, has enormous untapped potential for spreading the word about new products and services. But the most obvious application of public relations is its ability to promote people. Certainly America's Foremost Concert Sawist would pull out all the PR plugs in promoting his own album.

Entitled *There's a Song in My Saw*, the album went into distribution, and surprisingly, many record stores provided dramatic window displays for the oddball musical event. I would like to share with you the album jacket copy because it was written, not just to amuse the consumer, but to inspire and motivate the disc jockeys to read it on the air before or after they played a cut from the record. It shows that a public relations campaign can sometimes begin with the copy on a label:

> At last—beautiful music with some teeth in it—featuring America's foremost concert sawist, Robert C. Pritikin. Mr. Pritikin brings to the popular classics a musical, magic sawsory that cuts through all tradition.
>
> When Gene DeSmidt sings Mr. Pritikin's original melody, "There's a Song in My Saw," the melancholy wail of the saw reaches octaves almost inaudible to the human ear. You may be well advised to lock your dog in the garage.
>
> Mr. Pritikin engages a violin bow to produce his haunting sounds. And rarely has he stroked his instrument with more skill and virtuosity than on this collector's album. Into its third printing, *There's a Song in My Saw* is expected to sell well over a hundred copies and be a favorite for years to come.
>
> Mr. Pritikin is indeed among the great musical talents of our time, and it is regrettable that this, his finest album, is his last. Because when he cut this album, he inadvertently cut off his left leg.
>
> SIDE ONE: There's a Song in My Saw; Song Sawn Blue; The Last Time I Sawed Paris; Moonlight Sawnata; Sawdust.
>
> SIDE TWO: I Left My Heart in Saw Francisco; Sawmertime; Sawthing; I Sawed Mommy Kissing Santa Claus; When You Wish Upon a Saw.

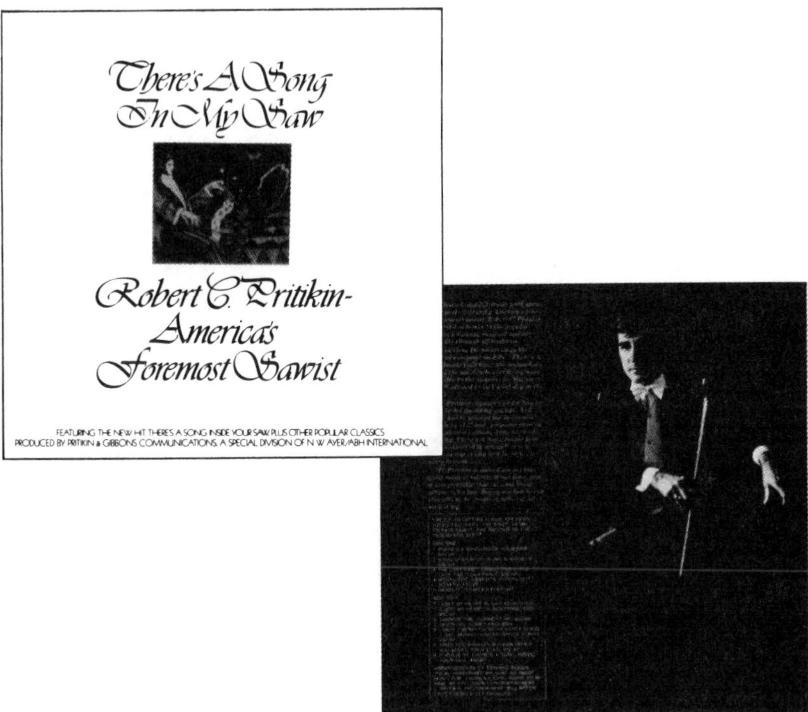

A number of disc jockeys read the album copy in its entirety on the air, tantamount to a free radio commercial for the album as was each air play of each selection on the record. San Francisco's KABL radio sponsored a three week on-the-air promotion inviting their listeners to send in suggested titles for Mr. Pritikin's next album. The promotional spots appeared every other hour on this AM/FM station, generating hundreds of responses. The punster who won the contest contributed more than a thousand titles. The radio station contributed the equivalent of thousands of dollars in "advertising" time to promote my album, at no cost to me or the distributors.

Disc Jockey Terry McGovern, headliner personality on KSAN, another San Francisco radio station, also jumped on the sawband wagon. He decided he would sponsor and host a continuing KSAN sawminar where I would preside over live on-the-air saw sawditions. The objective: to form the world's first saw band (band saw?). This zany promotion brought dozens of fledgling saw players out of the woodwork and provided even more PR (free advertising) to support my album sales in the stores.

Those were marvelous, madcap days. The bottom line, of course, is: how many albums were sold? I don't recall ever getting a clear accounting (watch out for record distributors), but my guess is about 10,000—a modest achievement by star standards, and it delivered only a modest profit, considering the PR effort I put behind it. The day the truck arrived at my house and disgorged 50 cases of unsold albums, I knew the party was over. Or was it?

Years before, *Playboy* magazine selected my apartment to appear as the Playboy Pad of the Month, in a five-page, full-color feature. I remembered that Tom Owen, the Modern Living Editor of *Playboy*, who supervised the exploitation of my apartment, was also in charge of the magazine's section called "*Playboy* Potpourri," which was subtitled in each issue, "People, Places, Objects and Events of Interest or Amusement." Perhaps Tom would find my album of sufficient interest or amusement? In the issue in which the story on my apartment had appeared, the *Playboy* Potpourri had featured a porn machine for $195 that blinked out four-letter words at random from a library of 8,000 possibilities on readout tubes; a huge plexiglass devil's face for $95 to be affixed to the hood of your auto; and a cookbook for $1.95 by underground comic R. Crumb, entitled *Eat It!* Would not *There's a Song in My Saw* have equally bizarre appeal? Talk about free advertising—*Playboy*'s Potpourri is literally that, because not only do they underwrite the art and production costs of the full-color "ads," but they list the price of the item and provide their vast reading audience with an address so that they may purchase the merchandise. The address could be my garage, which was warehousing thousands of my distressed albums.

Tom Owen elected to provide *Playboy* editorial space to present my silly record album to its 20 million readers. *Playboy* has given me permission to reproduce the minifeature.

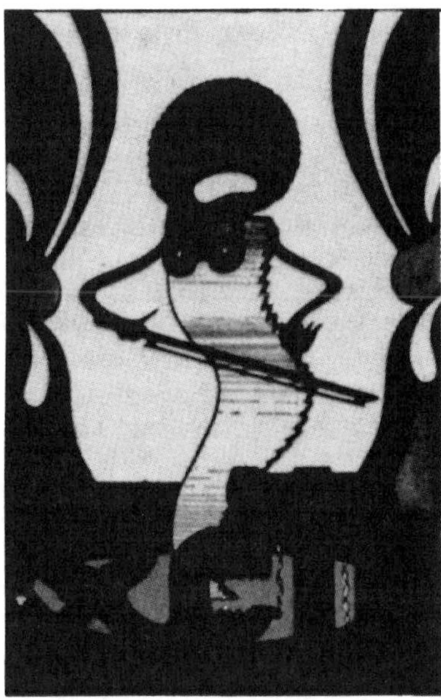

CUTTING AN LP

Besides living in a genuine Playboy Pad (PLAYBOY, June 1973), Robert C. Pritikin happens to be our top concert sawist. Sawist? Uh-huh. Pritikin, who makes his old woodcutter sound like a coloratura soprano, gets backing from the San Francisco Symphony string section and the Edwin Hawkins Singers as he cuts his way through some easy-listening standards on an LP, *There's a Song Inside Your Saw*. For your copy, send $4.98 to Saw, 2151 Sacramento Street, San Francisco 94109. It's sawmething else.

Art appeared in full color.

The checks poured in, and wasn't it fun! There were no middlemen, no distributors, certainly no advertising costs, and there was no cut for the retailer. I kept it all. But the impact of the *Playboy* story had hardly begun. Remember the thesis: "PR begets PR begets PR begets PR," etc.

For months after the *Playboy* blurb, I was besieged with phone calls from radio stations around the country and the world, DJs and talk-show hosts requesting on-the-air interviews with America's Foremost Classical Sawist. The East Coast morning commute shows were the most stressful. If I were scheduled for an 8:30 morning show in Boston, I would be obliged to be glib and witty at 5:30 A.M. San Francisco time. Try getting up at 5 A.M., a Central American army still marching in your mouth, not having seen or spoken to a single human, and then being plunged before an invisible audience of 100,000 commuters 3,000 miles away. While sometimes I did not field the interview with the wit and style I would have preferred, I never neglected to inform the listeners that by writing to SAW, 2151 Sacramento Street, San Francisco, and enclosing their check they would receive their very own autographed copy of *There's a Song in My Saw*. PR is a curious euphemism for this marvelous mass communication tool. More appropriate would be the letters FA-for Free Advertising!

Do not be reluctant to create advertising with the specific objective of having the advertising *itself* generate news coverage. After the city of San Francisco had been wallpapered with the visage of Hastings model Scott MacKenzie, it was time to double the value of the client's advertising dollars by engaging the news media to report on the advertising campaign. I am not referring to the advertising trade news media, such as *Adweek* or *Advertising Age*, but rather to the broad-based mass media that are addressed to the consumer. There are few advertising professionals who would give such PR much hope and accordingly they rarely make the effort on behalf of their clients. Because advertising writers and creative directors rarely even think of public relations, it is unlikely they would actually create advertising to have PR-able characteristics.

The advertising hacks and PR flacks were incredulous when their morning *San Francisco Chronicle* arrived on their doorsteps. Fully one-quarter of the front page (front page, mind you!) headlined, with photo, SEXIEST MODEL IN TOWN. If that were not enough, the story continued to page 6 of the main news section, where the entire page was given over to the Hastings advertising campaign. A banner head on that page read, HOW HASTINGS UPDATED ITS IMAGE—not exactly hard news, hardly news at all. Advertising experts, too quick to decide what is and isn't news, deny their clients marvelous opportunities for extensive free exposure.

Now Hastings would merely sit back and wait for the phone to ring, bringing the inevitable additional news activity following on the heels of the big newspaper story. The first call was from a local television channel. Tony Eglin, Hastings' ad manager at the time, and I wound up on prime time news for an eight-minute interview discussing the Hastings advertising campaign. At the present rate of $3,000 per commercial minute, that news interview addressing 333,000 people was worth $24,000, but Hastings got it free. Come to think of it, it was worth more than $24,000 because it was not advertising—it was *news*. I would give that single exposure a dollar value of $40,000.

The television news coverage ignited more coverage, which begat even more, and on and on.

I will share with you a cunning little scheme from which you may wish to extract principles applicable to your own PR needs. I recommended that my client, Hastings, spend a maximum of $500 to expose a radio commercial a couple of times on a single FM station. It was not the purpose of the radio commercial to advertise the wares of Hastings but rather to create a situation that would once again get them newspaper and TV news exposure.

The commercial invited the listener to send in $10 for the purchase of a full-size (12 feet x 25 feet) billboard of the famed Hastings model, Scott MacKenzie. The suggestion was made that the outsized supergraphic photograph be wallpapered to one's bedroom wall or ceiling. After about a dozen requests, the radio spot was terminated, and a press release was sent to the news media. It was the expectation that the TV cameras would move into the bedroom of a young lady, ga-ga over Scott MacKenzie, as she was posting the huge bulletin on her interior walls. We would even have Scott present to autograph the walls. Sure enough, the press bit, and heavy news coverage reported the non-event.

Much of what you see in the news is carefully orchestrated in advance. Some of the most skillful PR people, for instance, are those social dissidents whose marches and demonstrations are carefully sculpted, rehearsed, timed and choreographed to ensure the widest possible exposure.

There are few advertising people around who create advertising for the specific purpose of generating PR. While on the surface such a tactic may seem to be a convoluted approach to mass commercial communication exposure, when engineered with care and determination the technique can quadruple the value of an advertiser's dollars.

Without the resources of TV, radio, magazines, billboards, and the like, Jesus managed to "broadcast" his message to "all creation." He simply engaged the fundamental techniques of basic PR. Had he had, in addition, the modern facilities of print and broadcast to persuade and excite the multitudes, could he just possiby have saved himself so untimely a fate?

CHAPTER IX

AND THE BLIND WILL SEE: STARE WITH YOUR EARS AT RADIO

Most people who write radio write wrong radio. Of all mass media, radio is the most abused, the most misused. That's because most copywriters are blind—or perhaps deaf—to the potential of this magnificent medium. Their radio commercials go in one ear and out the same ear. The trouble is that radio commercials should not go in the ear at all, but in the eye.

Many have said—but few seem to have heeded—the cliché that radio at its most effective is a "visual medium." In the olden, golden days of radio, people sat down and "watched" their radio sets just as they watch their television screens today. Almost as Jesus gave sight to the blind, the miracle of radio once painted the most marvelous pictures for those who couldn't see. It's worth a look at those golden days to remind today's writers that there's more to radio than meets the ear.

I was presented a handsomely packaged album containing six records called *The First Fifty Years of Radio.* To my utter delight, the record that highlights the decade of the sixties features a radio commercial (the only commercial in the entire album collection) that I wrote way back when for the Fuller Paint Company.

That radio commercial was one in a series designed to paint dazzling colors on the screen of the listener's imagination. It blended music effects and word pictures into a statement that I believe is far more graphic than could ever have been achieved in the more literal pages of a magazine or, for that matter, on a television screen. Take a "look" at the words in that old radio commercial:

> The Fuller Paint Company invites you to stare with your ears at...yellow. Yellow is more than just a color. Yellow is a way of life. Ask any taxi driver about yellow. Or a banana salesman. Or a coward. They'll tell you about yellow. (PHONE RINGS) Oh, excuse me. Yello! Yes, I'll take your order. Dandelions, a dozen; a pound of melted butter; lemon drops and a drop of lemon; and one canary that sings a yellow song. Anything else? (CALLER HANGS UP) Yello? Yello? Yello? Oh, disconnected. Well, she'll call back. If you want yellow that's yellow-yellow, remember to remember the Fuller Paint Company, a century of

leadership in the chemistry of color. For the Fuller Color Center nearest you, check your phone directory. The yellow pages, of course.

This commercial and the other eight in the series were orchestrated with improvisational jazz and featured the haunting voice of Chicago's super-talented announcer, Ken Nordine. The campaign had some unique characteristics that delivered a two dollar media value for every dollar spent. Here's why.

The commercials were monitored as they were aired on the local stations. After the recorded commercial was completed, in some 50 percent of the cases, the station announcer, or DJ hosting the show, would proceed to rhapsodize about the commercial—its creativity, its unique use of radio as a medium, whatever came to his mind, for an average of twenty seconds. This free editorial comment had the effect of extending the commercials' sixty second length, for which the client paid, to eighty seconds or more. A DJ in Los Angeles was so enamored with one of the spots that he instructed his engineer to play the remaining eight in a row.

But there were other bonuses as well. Before the campaign was launched, radio time salesman from dozens of stations were given a preview of the campaign. All wished it for their radio stations for two reasons: First, they wanted to sell the air time; second, they were so startled and pleased at the creative content that they simply wanted their stations to be selected to air the spots. The reps were given two weeks to come up with promotional schemes to support the campaign and advised that only half the station reps convened would be awarded the business. The station salesmen returned with such on-air promotions as Paint the Town Red Week, Yellow Tuesdays, and so forth. This free promo activity further extended the mileage of the client's dollars. But most important was the impact and attention the commercials received from the average listener. The Fuller Paint Company was deluged with mail from its regular customers and new customers so delighted by the refreshing change in paint advertising that they promised to switch their brands. A Sinclair Paint Company store manager in Studio City complained that he had to remove his radio from his store because whenever a Fuller Paint commercial came on he couldn't sell his own brand of paint. It wasn't because his customers were listening to the radio; they were watching it and seeing his competitor's colors.

When you write a radio commercial for the eye, instead of for the ear, you can expect to achieve enormous recall value. The most elementary memory course will teach you that to remember something, you must visualize it, and if you can provide action with the visual, you can further extend the recall process. What's more, if you can make the visual a bit out of the ordinary, even bizarre (providing it is relevant), greater recall will result.

If you are of the age, you will remember the Green Hornet and the Lone Ranger and the marvelous Arch Oboler radio shows. Didn't you know exactly what Jack, Doc and Reggie looked like in *I Love A Mystery;* and Chi-Chi and Papa David in *Life Can Be Beautiful?* Next time you write for radio or judge a radio commercial, keep in mind the lessons of these old radio classics. You can go so much further to stretch the imagination when you project your pictures on the private screen of your listener's imaginings: You can build sets to dwarf Spielberg's most extravagant creations. You can conjure up the beauty of a Garbo, the fantasies of a Jonathan Swift. Your words can paint watches melting, armies marching and angels in flight.

But your client will say no. He wants his product to be seen. Tell your client that it will be seen as never before, and remembered all the way to the sales rack, the grocer's shelf or the showroom floor, because great radio is *always* seen and never heard.

Just a few reminders before you take pen (and paint brush) in hand. When you write radio for the eye, you must know the magic of words. You must know that verbs are more visible than adjectives, and that a silent pause can be the most dramatic language of all. And you must know that a minute can be a span in geologic time into which the history of man can be compressed, or a minute can be a microscope to focus on a speck of sand.

Perhaps a psychologist could best explain the phenomenon of radio and its incomparable potential to carve deep recollective impressions. I believe it has to do with the fact that the listener is required to create his own mental pictures. Great radio is not a passive experience as television often is. The great radio writers, including those who write commercials, paint only part of the picture. The writer provides clues, lays down the broad strokes delineating the subject and the point of view. It is the listener who paints in the details. And, as in any other activity requiring active participation and involvement, the experience holds more meaning and is remembered longer. What's the key to writing great radio? Engage the listener as your co-author.

Perhaps radio has the broadest potential of all mass communications media because radio can reach the senses as no other medium can. Of course, radio is pictorial, and in the grandest sense. But can it not with equal effectiveness reach the olfactory, the tactile and the taste senses as well? With its unique capacity to conjure and cajole, radio can open your senses to fragrance, feeling and taste. Give me a few mouth-watering words and the sound of fire and steam, and I will hand you a succulent steak right through your radio speaker.

But the everlasting pity is that this extraordinary device, developed by Guglielmo Marconi in 1895, is still to this day mostly engaged to appeal only to hearing—the one human sense it is least effective in reaching.

I have discovered a radio commercial that, in my judgment, is the world's worst radio commercial, and I would like to share it with you. The commercial was part of a continuing campaign by northern California's Comfort Zone Waterbed stores. If one purpose of a radio commercial is to reflect the essence of a product, and if the purpose of a waterbed is to provide a peaceful night's sleep or other nocturnal pleasures, one wonders why Comfort Zone's advertising is such a nightmare of shouting, screaming and harassment.

The reason I treasure this awful commercial is because I was invited to create a counter-campaign by their competitor, Body Comfort Waterbeds.

Apparently the advertising counsel who wrote the radio spot for Comfort Zone felt that a picture is *not* worth a thousand words, and in fact elected to squeeze what seems like a thousand words into the sixty-second radio commercial time parameter.

(As you read on, you will find it increasingly difficult to distinguish my client, Body Comfort Waterbeds, from my competitor, Comfort Zone Waterbeds, because of the similarity in their names. I'm not sure who came first, but may I suggest that if you form a retail company or are engaged to name one, you first research your competitors' names and select a name that cannot be confused with your adversary in the marketplace.)

In the next pages of this book—side by side, double-truck as we say in advertising—you will see the commercial scripts for the competitor, Comfort Zone, and our client, Body Comfort. You will note that the Comfort Zone script on the left side is more than twice as long as the Body Comfort script for my client on the right side.

Comfort Zone has, in fact, squeezed 227 words into sixty seconds. Since this book is in print instead of on audio tape, I implore you to conduct a private experiment. Sit down with

Comfort Zone's script in front of a clock with a second hand and read it and reread it until you can race through this marathon of words in precisely sixty seconds. Only this way will you appreciate what the commercial actually sounds like on the air.

Now I might add that there are very few commercial announcers who can accomplish this *Guinness Book of World Records* feat. John Moschitta, famed for his fast-speech Federal Express commercials, could have done it, but his technique is used for satire or comedy. Comfort Zone came up with a guy who could machine gun their words and they were not attempting comedy.

If you are of the school of thought that the more words you can compress into your radio commercial the more value it has, you may be interested to know that an electronic device has been invented that permits a commercial announcer to record a minute and a half of commercial copy, which can then be squeezed into sixty seconds without altering the pitch of the announcer's voice. It's used all the time—often, I suspect, altering the sanity of the listener.

Our competitor, Comfort Zone, engaged a single announcer with no music, no special effects. Our radio campaign also engaged a single announcer, the late Paul Frees, whose voice was an instrument of genius and whose interpretive skills could put goose bumps on your goose bumps. We also added some gentle music and a short musical vocal introduction and musical vocal close. Yes, it takes more time to sing a word than to speak it, but the opening and closing lyric only required a total of twenty-six sung words, or seventeen seconds.

Please read both commercials. (Don't forget to read Comfort Zone's commercial to a second hand and don't give up until you deliver it in precisely sixty seconds.) Read my commercial in thirty-nine seconds because the singing lyric requires twenty-one seconds. You should get the picture—that radio should be a picture.

(COMFORT ZONE WATERBEDS)
60 SECONDS

READ IN SIXTY SECONDS

ANNOUNCER: Wow! It is exciting—the Comfort Zone Waterbed warehouse, and we're here, seventeen, the Nimitz and Fremont Boulevard, right next to General Motors. But look at these prices. How 'bout a complete six-piece bedroom suite? You get it all, too—the Barker six-piece suite. Deluxe headboard, the dresser, two mirrors, two night stands—two hundred and ninety-nine dollars for everything, ready to go. And look at these waterbeds right now! If you're looking for a beautiful waterbed—these prices—there are so many beds under two hundred dollars with top quality and I mean Comfort Zone reputation. The Comfort Zone Waterbed, for example, starting at eighty-eight dollars, solid two by ten construction. You get the solid wood base, pedestal, safety liner, thermostat control heater, the Chemolex thirty-three B, the Hodel water mattress, we feel the finest in the industry, everything for eighty-eight dollars. But what about that beautiful padded waterbed—a king-sized padded waterbed ready to go complete for one forty-eight. Or the four-poster waterbed for one-seventy-seven. And that beautiful Winchester—the bookcase headboard, where you can put your clock radio, pictures, whatever you want to in the bookcase headboard, a complete waterbed—one eighty-eight. But get over here—satin comforters for eighteen dollars, and there's more. Seventeen, the Nimitz at Fremont Boulevard before ten tonight. The Comfort Zone.

(BODY COMFORT WATERBEDS)
60 SECONDS

READ ALL ANNOUNCER COPY
IN THIRTY-NINE SECONDS

MUSIC: GENTLE-CONTEMPORARY

ANNOUNCER: Your most treasured possession—it is your body.

MUSIC—VOCAL: COMFORT YOUR BODY
IN A BODY COMFORT WATERBED
WHAT A BEAUTIFUL WAY
TO LAY YOUR BODY DOWN

ANNOUNCER: Every single day—your body has the opportunity to engage in a marvelous, sensual, almost spiritual experience. It is called sleep. Body Comfort Waterbed is *the* distinguished name in waterbeds. They helped pioneer the important advances in waterbed comfort. And, take comfort in this: at Body Comfort there's a thirty-day trial guarantee. Open every day 'til ten and you get the lowest possible prices commensurate with the highest quality. Perhaps you should spend that important one-third of your life in a Body Comfort Waterbed.

GENTLE VOCAL: WHAT A BEAUTIFUL WAY
TO LAY YOUR BODY DOWN

ANNOUNCER TAG: Take 101 to Whipple or Holly exit on Industrial Road just north of Circle Star Theatre.

Radio is a very intimate, one-to-one medium. And advertising is an idiom of selling. Can you imagine a salesperson, who is expected to have some charm and restraint as well as persuasion, approaching you face to face with the kind of frenzied pitch necessary to condense 231 words into sixty seconds? Why, if you ever encountered such a person in real life, you would either run in terror or phone the authorities to cart him off to the booby hatch.

The little gentle commercial for Body Comfort beat the pants off the Comfort Zone commercial and supported once again my ardent conviction that a whisper is more audible than a shout and that a picture is indeed worth more than a thousand words.

I was engaged by Bill McGee, a gravelly, old-trapper kind of guy who grew up in the broadcasting sales business and formed a company called Broadcast Marketing, to write a film. The movie was supposed to persuade retail stores like Macy's or Bloomingdale's or chains of auto supply stores and stereo stores to switch some of their advertising dollars over from newspaper, their traditional friend, to radio.

I took on the assignment with a certain glee because I knew how impossible the task would be and I was excited with the challenge of moving advertising dollars from newsprint into the less tangible medium of radio airwaves. McGee has informed me since that the film, *Get It On Radio*, is specifically credited with moving over $50 million from newsprint to radio. Nonetheless, I am a devotee of newspaper advertising. And newspaper advertising will have its day in an upcoming chapter. Meanwhile, we are talking about radio, so in this chapter radio will star.

There are hundreds of thousands of retail stores, spending tens of billions on mass madia advertising each year. Retailer, you own the huge supermarket chains, the department stores, the clothing emporiums, the stop-smoking clinics, the video stores, the small stereo chains, the furniture stores, the gift shops and specialty outlets for every object and service imaginable. Retailers, why are you so frightened of radio? It won't bite you. Why do you dump all or most of your advertising dollars into newsprint? Did you see your last ad, buried there at the bottom of the page next to that small space ad selling a hemorrhoid cure? Your ad looked gorgeous on the drawing board, didn't it? Good strong blacks, bold white? What happened when it wound up in the newspaper? You say it all turned gray?

In the next chapter I'll show you how to make your newspaper ads work a lot better. But you have to promise that you'll accept a gift. It's a gift of a free radio advertising campaign. There's a way you can purchase a schedule of radio time on your local stations and it won't cost you an extra nickel.

The first thing you do is shrink your newspaper ads. Shrink them all by 25 percent. You need not lose a single reader for your smaller ads because they will have more impact and they will be more visible. If you are now spending $100,000 a year on newspaper advertising space, you will have released $25,000 to get your feet wet in radio.

A compilation of thousands of ad studies taken from Starch-Indra-Hooper research shows that if you reduce the size of a newspaper ad as much as 50 percent, you will sacrifice only about 26 percent of your readership. But with the techniques I will show you in a subsequent chapter, especially written for the retailer, you not only won't lose any readers, you'll gain new ones.

Radio is virtually the only medium where production costs can be absolutely free. In print you have the expense of setting type, art and layout costs, photostats and so forth. In television you have the horrendous costs of film or tape production, although there are some TV stations that will give you a cheap tape commercial if you purchase enough time.

But if you use a live radio announcer to deliver your radio commercial, you do not spend a nickel for production. All you need are your words on a piece of paper for him to read. It can even be simpler—many stations are delighted to work from a fact sheet. Just write one and the announcer will ad lib his way through the sixty seconds. Shrink your ads down and channel the money you save into radio. It won't cost you any extra money and you may be amazed at the results you achieve.

If you start to feel good about it, the next creative plateau is a recorded radio commercial. It can't have the personal touch of the live delivery, but it could have more impact and persuasion because you have total control of every inflection, every nuance in the announcers' delivery. If it's appropriate and cost-efficient, you can also include music and effects.

My assignment was to write a cheapo radio commercial for Quinn's Lighthouse restaurant in Oakland. The restaurant sits on a dock and much of the pleasure in going there is the atmosphere. The food's good, too.

Any local recording studio has a collection of sound-effects records, which, of course, include foghorns and splashing water. I availed myself of this inexpensive audio atmosphere and hired a velvet voice to read my sensual, mouth-watering copy. Now I want you to read this commercial slowly *and* read it out loud. Poetry and radio commercials should never be read silently. After you finish reading it, see if you don't *feel* the atmosphere of Quinn's Lighthouse as well as savor the beautiful food. And ask yourself if you could have achieved that same level of persuasion in the gray pages of your local fish wrap.

SOUND EFFECTS IN BACKGROUND:
WATER, CREAKING BOATS, AND QUIET FOGHORNS
HEARD THROUGHOUT.

VELVET VOICE ANNOUNCER: There's a kind of unreality in the old lighthouse. Quinn's Lighthouse on the Oakland estuary. It's a restaurant now. And the legendary lighthouse still creaks just like the boats outside. And sometimes the people who dine in this marvelous and remote sanctuary claim to hear the voice of Lightkeeper Quinn in the whirr of the ceiling fans. Place your order, won't you? Steamed clams. Giant shrimp sautéed in wine. Or a combination of steak and lobster combined with the sound of the sea. For lunch or dinner or weekend brunch—Quinn's Lighthouse at 1951 Embarcadero. Driving south? Take the Nimitz to Sixteenth Avenue Exit North—take Fifth Avenue Exit. If you hunger for great food and a very special adventure, remember Quinn's Lighthouse, on the Oakland estuary.

Retailers, arise! Open your eyes! You've been blind too long to the dramatic potential of radio for selling your goods and services. Shrink the size of your newspaper ads and turn yourself on. To radio.

CHAPTER X

THE WORD ACCORDING TO MATTHEW, MARK, LUKE AND JOHN

The New Testament of Jesus Christ is the greatest printed advertisement of all time. The King James version has effectively sold its proposition for hundreds of years to tens of millions of people. An advertising man would do well to study it for its provocative "headlines" and pithy parables that Christ created and his disciples recorded.

Certainly Christ knew the verve of a verb, the sting of a single syllable, the power of language that is pure and simple.

The light of the body is the eye.

Out of thine own mouth will I judge thee.

The wages of sin is death.

Those ad headline writers who think "Summertime Is Sandwich Time" will command interest at the top of an ad should study the greatest ad man of all, whose "headlines" didn't beg for attention—they demanded it. So provocative were his thoughts, so graphic his language that even the most cynical, the staunchest disbelievers had to stop and listen. If you open the Gospel according to St. Matthew, St. Mark, St. Luke or St. John, you will open new insights learned from the Master himself.

Today the onmipresence of print advertising is staggering and, often, suffocating: magazine ads, newspaper ads, booklets, brochures, direct mail, annual reports, hanging store banners, window display cards, shelf talkers, outdoor billboards, posters, bumper stickers, retail rack displays, letterheads, business cards, transit ads, shopping bags, calendars, pencils, matchbooks, labels, T-shirts, campaign buttons, shirt cardboards, mimeograph handouts, balloons, and more, more, more. When Gutenberg first invented movable type, he had in mind printing words. But his extraordinary invention spawned the printing of many things besides words. Now we print in three dimensions; we print sound; we print fragrance. And we can print on virtually anything, including the delicate shell of an egg.

If the printed word and the printed picture have sufficient strength, they can be recorded for the life span of any man in the secret underfolds of his mind.

Each printed medium imposes its own restraints and challenges. There is no doubt in my mind that the 50,000 plus words in this book could be reorganized to discuss the single topic of matchbook cover advertising. This chapter presents but a few case histories, concentrating on magazines and newspapers. But if there are any insights to be enjoyed, please apply them cautiously and selectively to every consideration of print communications, perhaps even including that special yearning to carve a heart and a few initials on an old oak tree.

When you create an advertisement for magazines or newspapers, you should remind yourself of three areas of competition. First, you will be competing for attention and readership with all other ads in the newspaper or publication that are *within your product category.* (If you are Coca-Cola, for example, you may consider all ingestible liquids competitors.) The second area of competition is *all* other ads in the publication. This chapter, like the others, is not concerned simply with producing adequate professional advertising, but rather with producing *extraordinary* advertising, and so I refer you to a third area of competition, the *editorial* content of the publication.

Regarding the last, if your ad is to appear in a newsweekly, you may be competing for attention and readership with an impending international drug war or a breakthrough treatment for AIDS or some loonie taking a potshot at the Pope. If your ad were to appear in *People* magazine, you could be competing with the latest celebrity scandal or the birth of a two-headed goat. Notwithstanding those few who will read every word on every page, your ad, unless it is devastating in its impact, may not stand a chance.

As of this writing, a full-color, full-page ad in the national issue of *People* costs $66,000; a full-color page in *Newsweek* is $134,360; the back cover of *Playboy* is $109,240, a half page in the *New York Sunday Times* is $20,980, and a full black-and-white page in *Farm Journal* is $34,400. This chapter is intended to show you how to get as much readership for your ad as editorial material about Princess Di or Michael Jackson or Hillary Clinton or a visitor from Mars would get. Well, maybe not that much readership.

Your advertising headline should be as arresting, as provocative, as the headlines that attract the reader into the editorial copy—even more so. It might be helpful if you were reminded of some of the headlines that induce readers into news and editorial copy in *Time* magazine. And lest you think I am dramatizing only the best of *Time* headlines, I should tell you that all of these editorial headlines are taken from a single issue that I selected at random. As you read these headlines and their subheads, just imagine how much impact your advertising headlines would have to have in order to compete for readership.

FLIBBERTIGIBBET—Looking For Work

HOT PROSPECT—Off Alaska's Frigid Shores

ANOTHER OIL PRICE STUNNER

GIZMOS TO SAVE ENERGY: THE COOLING OF AMERICA
'Twas The Night Before Christmas,
And All Through The House: Brrr!

THE ARMY REARS UP

...AND A FISH IN A FIR TREE

THE STRANGE CASE OF "DR. DUNK"

FRAGRANCE WAR: FRANCE VS. U.S.

THE POOR SUFFER THE MOST

At a cost of $150,000 per national color advertising page, you would certainly think the advertisers would come up with headlines at least as titillating as those inviting the reader to scan the dreary news. Not so. In that very same issue of *Time*, the following boring, banal headlines appeared over full-page advertisements:

For Johnny Walker:
THIS TIME OF YEAR,
THERE'S NOTHING AS TRADITIONAL AS RED

For NBC:
SEE ALL THE ACTION ON NBC RADIO

For Merit Cigarettes:
MERIT WINS CHOICE TEST

For True:
UNEXPECTED TASTE

For Vantage:
WHERE GREAT TASTE AND LOW TAR MEET

For Webster's Dictionary:
A GIFT FILLED WITH MEANING—
GIVE THE DICTIONARY THAT WORKS!

For Bayer:
FOR ACHES AND FEVER OF COLDS AND FLU,
ALL YOU NEED IS BAYER ASPIRIN

For Early Times Bourbon:
THE WAY IT WAS, THE WAY IT IS

For Seagram's Whiskey:
SYMBOL OF THE QUALITY GIFT

At the very least, one would hope that in *Time*'s Christmas issue the advertisers would give us a gift of interesting headlines. At the very most, one would think they would give themselves the advantage of arresting, competitive, persuasive advertising. No, instead the cigarette, wine, and liquor people spent more than $2,000,000—almost 70 percent of the total full-and half-page color ads in the publication—to remind us once again that the creative advertising product of America's largest advertising agencies and their huge clients is usually an abysmal bore as well as an enormous waste of money. Imagine the headline SYMBOL OF A QUALITY GIFT competing for readership with THE STRANGE CASE OF "DR. DUNK."

Most advertising copywriters would be well-advised to apprentice with one of New York's tabloids where headline writing has been elevated to an art form and the highest level of sleaze. Mike Pearl of the *New York Post*, a master headliner himself, cites two of his favorites:

HEADLESS BODY IN TOPLESS BAR

*****

SHE WAS NICE TO ME—THEN I KICKED HER OFF THE ROOF

How unfortunate that advertisements rarely have the pithy punch of a good tab headline. "THREE PEOPLE KILLED IN DOG PLUNGE." What a marvelous and provocative idea—followed by the lead paragraph, "A dog that fell from a 13th floor balcony Friday night triggered three deaths here, police and witnesses said." Most advertising copywriters need an elementary course in journalism to be reminded of the five W's: Who, What, Where, When, and Why.

It's the hot, staccato monosyllabics that make for great headlines. It's the verve! It's the verbs! The last good headline for Campbell Soup that I read was in the main news section of the *San Francisco Chronicle.* And it wasn't an ad; it was a news story. The headline—CAMPBELL SOUP IN HOT WATER—was followed by the the sub-head *Deceptive Ads Alleged.*

Put a hot headline on top of your ad and you can get ten times the readership in one-tenth the space. POLAR BEARS KILL CHILDREN IN BROOKLYN ZOO. MODEL KILLED BY CROCODILE. ROCK HUDSON GOES STRAIGHT IN AFTERLIFE. YOUR SHOE SIZE TELLS HOW LONG YOU'LL LIVE. LONELY COUPLE KEEPS THEIR KID IN DIAPERS FOR 25 YEARS. TEEN CASTRATES SELF WHEN PARENTS WON'T TAKE HIM TO THE ZOO! Here are some lulus from the Weekly World News:

BABY BORN WITH WOODEN LEG

DEAD MAN'S HEART
STARTED WITH JUMPER CABLES

ONE HEAD WANTS A GIRL—THE OTHER A BOY
2-HEADED WOMAN:
"I'M PREGNANT"

HUMAN BLIMP
POPS LIKE BALLOON

PET ROOSTER PULLS
DROWNING CHILD
FROM ICY POND

You say such provocative headlines *cannot* be created for Toyota, Dewar's White Label, Contadina Tomato Sauce, Macy's, Stove Top Stuffing Mix, or Apple Computer. You say quite wrong.

My client managed to raise $5,000 to introduce a new product named Changing Times throughout Northern California. His goal was to create widespread distribution in department stores and retail outlets; and perhaps even incite the news media to report on his new product. A lovely and grandiose objective for a total advertising budget of $5,000 that surely would not even cover my fee.

Because it was the Christmas season, I took on the task with a giving spirit and a certain creative attitude. I determined that $5,000 would purchase fifteen small space one-column four-inch ads in the *San Francisco Chronicle/Examiner* and five billboards. If ever blockbuster headlines were needed it was now. Here are some of those headlines as they appeared in bold type on billboards.

NUCLEAR MELTDOWN ON NOB HILL

*****

GAY JEWS FOR JESUS. JOIN NOW!

*****

SAN FRANCISCO METER MAIDS SOLD FOR BONDAGE.

*****

While the *Chronicle*'s full-page, half-page and expensive display ads all screamed out in their typographical frenzy for the reader's attention, their collective cacophony could not compete with the postage stamp ad whose headline proclaimed SAN FRANCISCO METER MAIDS SOLD FOR BONDAGE and whose signature simply stated CHANGING TIMES.

A press release invited the broadcast and print news media to learn about Changing Times. There was much speculation about this curious advertising campaign that was so teasing and titillating the community.

What exactly was Changing Times? Was it a bizarre cult? Was it a revolutionary publication of some sort? Changing Times was, in fact, a new board game—with some of the characteristics of the famed Parker Brothers' Monopoly. The game required that the players invent new social orders, however outlandish, and then play them out competitively with a throw of dice and a deck of special playing cards.

The provocative headlines were entirely relevant insofar as the player could produce any societal revolution his imagination could conjure.

The $5,000 advertising budget produced a news media blitz which, were the time and space purchased with advertising dollars, would have had a value of more than $150,000. The game achieved widespread distribution in hundreds of outlets and the consumers flocked to the department stores, the game stores and the discount outlets to get in on the fun.

SUMMERTIME IS SANDWICH TIME, indeed!

In the chapter on radio, I provided you with what in my view was the world's worst radio commercial. I will now introduce for your inspection what to my lights is the world's worst print ad. There are many "world's worst" print ads. Qualification for this distinction requires only that no other ad be any worse; hence, there can be many world's worst. Studying god-awful ads such as these on the following pages can be as instructive as studying brilliant ads. Read the Macy's ad carefully and determine for yourself why it never should have been run. I should mention this ad appeared in newspaper Sunday supplements as a full page in full expensive color.

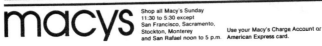

let your imagination take flight, your spirits soar.
introducing the firebird suite. a symphony of color, new from borghese

Improvise. Harmonize. Let your imagination take wing. Everything you need is here in one masterwork of fiery color, Borghese's stirring Firebird Suite. It's like a symphony in three movements. The introductory Firebird. The pulsing Allegro. And the breathtaking Arabesque as a finale. Colors to dazzle the eye and delight the senses. All, a soaring crescendo of color that builds from winged violet and feathered rose to a burst of fireplum and red of paradise. 4.50-8.50. Let a Borghese beauty expert give you a sneak preview of the collection at all Macy's Tuesday, March 11 through Saturday, March 15. (March 10 through March 15 at Macy's San Francisco.) And, as a special prelude to spring, get a beautiful Lumina bonus. A half ounce of Lumina Daytime Moisturizer and a half ounce of Lumina Radiant Finish Makeup, your gift with any Borghese purchase you make. Cosmetics (d. 76) - all Macy's

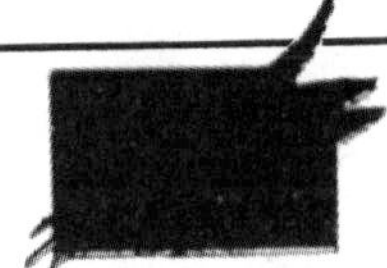

the firebird
Soaring. Scintillating. Yours in such spellbinding shades as Winged Violet, Teal Peacock, Plum Plume, Plum Piper, Paradise Red, Flamingo Gold and Firebird.

the allegro
A rousing rendering of brilliant color. Shades like Winged Pink, Purple Smoke, Fireplum, Plum Piper, Paradise Red, Flamingo Gold and Flamingo.

the arabesque
Breathtaking colors as light as flight. Choose from Feathered Rose, Pink Sunbird, Ostrich Brown, Plum Piper, Paradise Red, Flamingo Gold and Mulberry.

Shop all Macy's Sunday 11:30 to 5:30 except San Francisco, Sacramento, Stockton, Monterey and San Rafael noon to 5 p.m.

Use your Macy's Charge Account or American Express card.

The reason the Macy's ad is such an abomination is the reader has absolutely no idea what the ad is attempting to sell. Sheets? Cosmetics? Or what? And if cosmetics, what kind of cosmetics and for what purpose? The headline, LET YOUR IMAGINATION TAKE FLIGHT, is well advised because the reader would require quite a flight of imagination to understand what the ad is about in the first place. Copywriters who create such unctuous, saccharine exercises in literary masturbation should really be jerked off their jobs forthwith. One cannot imagine a greater waste of advertising dollars than running an ad in which the product and its use is drowned in a thick syrup of pretentious prose.

Gawdawful ads can be just as instructive as brilliant ads. The Corporate Lodging of Houston company, below, decided that a naked, dismembered manikin would be an appropriate symbol to sell corporate lodging. I have decided that this ad be nominated for the Hall of Infamy of the world's worst ads.

Paying an arm and a leg for a hotel room?
Then stay at Corporate Lodging, "the hotel alternative", on your next trip to Houston. Located near the Galleria, Westchase and Greenway Plaza, Corporate Lodging offers fully furnished apartment suites starting at $49/night. Each suite has a private line telephone, color TV, fully equipped kitchen and daily maid service. Recreational facilities include swimming, outdoor whirlpool and tennis. Whatever your pleasure, Corporate Lodging has it all.
Corporate Lodging of Houston
ADULT SECTION
6267 Westheimer
Houston, Texas 77057
(713) 780-7230
FAMILY SECTION
7979 Westheimer
R-001
Houston, Texas 77063
(713) 974-0401

While we are on the subject of disabled human bodies, let's study this New York Life ad which attempts to get our attention by displaying a contortionist who has twisted himself into a knot. I trust the twisted thinking copywriter who dreamed up this ad has not included it in his portfolio for a new job. I nominate this ad *not* for the Hall of Infamy—but for the Hall of Infancy.

If choosing between life insurance and competitive interest rates has you tied up in knots...
get them both.
Up to now, it's often been a case of one or the other. You could either buy life insurance protection for your family *or* put money away at competitive interest rates.
But now you can do both—with New York Life's new Target Life℠ policy.*
It is a life insurance plan that provides $100,000 or more of protection at low rates. At the same time, it is a plan to build funds for college, retirement, whatever your target.
Target Life provides remarkable flexibility within Internal Revenue Code requirements:
• You decide each year how much you can afford to put into the policy. There are no fixed payments.
• You decide how much goes into cash values, where it accumulates tax-sheltered at competitive rates.
• You can withdraw funds, vary the amount of protection or the amount of cash values, and even insure other family members on your one policy.
So our Target Life universal life policy not only keeps you from being tied up in knots, but makes planning your family's financial security a whole lot easier.
Why not get all the details today. Ask your New York Life Agent.
NEW YORK LIFE
"ASK ME."

Pall Mall should certainly know better than to okay the expenditure of God-knows-how-many hundreds of thousands of dollars for this non-sequitur ad that shows a giant pack of cigarettes bursting through the roof of a barn. Yes, Pall Mall, you qualify for my Hall of Insanity.

For puns carried to the third power, my World's Worst goes to the Las Vegas Convention and Visitors Authority. A newspaper advertisement should, at a glance, provide information about a product or service. A bottle of catsup is hardly a relevant symbol for the resort/vacation destination of Las Vegas. Come to think of it—maybe it is? This ad will hang in my Hall of Inane.

"Catch Up" On The Good Times.
LAS VEGAS
Las Vegas pours on the excitement 24 hours a day.
That's why more than twelve million people will add Las Vegas to their vacation and convention plans.
Las Vegas offers the world's greatest entertainers and lavish revues, served right before your table.
For your dining pleasure, choose from gourmet to buffet.
For the sport of it, play the first class tennis and golf facilities of Las Vegas.
Best of all, Las Vegas room rates rank among the least expensive in the resort industry.
So when you call your travel agent for your next vacation, tell them to serve you Las Vegas, in the large economy bottle.
The Resort Bargain of the World.

Las Vegas Convention and Visitors Authority

Next time you write an ad or judge an ad, consider the headline. If it is both relevant to the product sell and at the same time knocks you on your behind, you've probably got a winner.

As I reflect back on the many headlines I have written, one in particular comes to mind as perfectly meeting these two criteria. The full-page ad was created for a tiny California retail client, but it upstaged thousands of ads created for the multimillion-dollar advertising spenders by winning first place in the National Addy Awards sponsored by the American Advertising Federation. The headline was:

SHE HAS 18 BREASTS AND A DRAWER IN HER FOREHEAD.

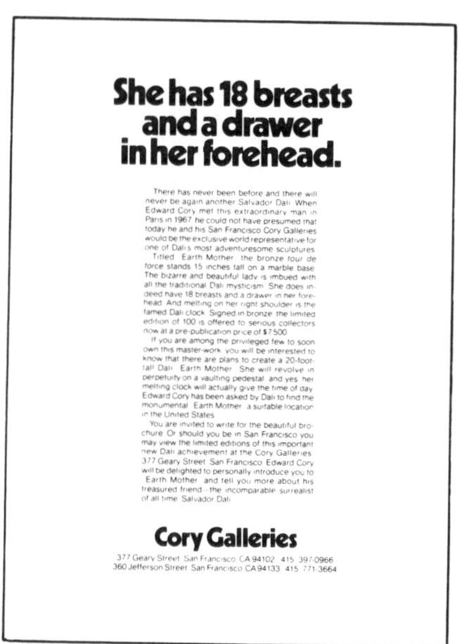

Consider, if you will, the stunning impact of that headline, set in 72 point sans serif ultra boldface type in the pages of a magazine or newspaper. Who could resist delving further into the text of that ad? But once you have grabbed your reader with such a headline device, you must then sustain the reader throughout the copy with relevant information. Do not ever deceive your reader by simply holding out tantalizing bait in the headline without ensuring there is credible follow through in the copy. In advertising lingo, this is called "borrowed interest;" in anyone else's language, it is just plain cheating.

SHE HAS 18 BREASTS AND A DRAWER IN HER FOREHEAD was an all-copy ad. I had the option of photographing the curious lady, but instead I elected to hold my cards close, at least until after the reader was enticed into the text of the ad and was sailing through the "sell."

Lest you be on pins and needles, here is the text of that ad:

SHE HAS 18 BREASTS
AND A DRAWER
IN HER FOREHEAD.

There has never been before and there will never be again another Salvador Dali. When Edward Cory met this extraordinary man in Paris in 1967, he could not have presumed that today he and his San Francisco Cory Galleries would be the exclusive world representative for one of Dali's most adventuresome sculptures.

Titled "Earth Mother," the bronze tour de force stands 15 inches tall on a marble base. The bizarre and beautiful lady is imbued with all the traditional Dali mysticism. She does indeed have 18 breasts and a drawer in her forehead. And melting on her right shoulder is the famed Dali clock. Signed in bronze, the limited edition of 100 is offered to serious collectors now at a prepublication price of $7,500.

If you are among the privileged few to soon own this masterwork, you will be interested to know that there are plans to create a 20-foot-tall Dali "Earth Mother." She will revolve in perpetuity on a vaulting pedestal; and yes, her melting clock will actually give the time of day. Edward Cory was asked by the late Salvador Dali to find the monumental "Earth Mother" a suitable location in the United States.

You are invited to write for a beautiful brochure. Or should you be in San Francisco you may view the limited editions of this important new Dali achievement at the Cory Galleries, 377 Geary Street, San Francisco. Edward Cory will be delighted to personally introduce you to "Earth Mother" and tell you more about his treasured friend—the incomparable surrealist of all time, Salvador Dali.

CORY GALLERIES

377 GEARY STREET, SAN FRANCISCO, CA 94102. (415) 397-0966
360 JEFFERSON STREET, SAN FRANCISCO, CA 94133. (415) 771-3664

I remember Michael Dacres Dixon as a man of consummate elegance. A Britisher of some vague royal lineage, he claimed a blood connection to the Dixon who was presumably shipped to early America to plot the Mason-Dixon line. Always bespectacled, and be-vested, and with an air of bemusement, to my knowledge he was never seen without a tiny, fresh rosebud in his lapel.

And if those trappings were not enough to separate him from the crowd, he had one more feature to guarantee his absolutely memorable visage: his right arm was missing, and the empty sleeve of his Oxford jacket was always impeccably tucked into his side coat pocket.

Dixon was president of Scotland's Scottish & Newcastle Company in charge of the distribution and marketing of Cluny Scotch in the U.S. He approached my associate, Jerry Gibbons, and me with a most challenging assignment: development of a complete marketing and advertising plan to introduce a new, yet-to-be-named wine from, of all places, Argentina.

To create a product where once there was none—to name it, label it, give it a personality, and then send it on its way—is a Frankensteinian process that can, and usually does, lead to a monster. The average supermarket displays some 25,000 different items. Each year tens of thousands of new products are created with the intention of bumping the old standbys off the shelf. Few of the new entries ever prove their worth in test marketing, and those that do rarely survive the real test of getting mass distribution followed by massive, continuing sales.

As I sat staring at my sample Bordeaux bottle containing the nameless Argentinian wine, I was ill-disposed to imagine how this upstart could ever successfully compete with the premium California varietals. True, it had performed admirably in blind tastings, and Michael Dixon, a wine aficionado with a highly civilized palate, was doggedly confident. But still—wine from Argentina?

That weekend I accepted an invitation from Los Angeles friends to lounge by their pool and get away from my woes about wine. At one end of the pool a large cage housed what looked to me to be some ornithological mutant—a scrawny, screaming creature whose feathers could have been transplanted from an old hat.

"What is it?" I asked my host.

"An Argentine Trumpeter," he replied.

Was it perhaps preordained that on that very weekend I be in the presence of that awful Argentinian fowl? Was the very identity of the new wine from Argentina somehow interlaced with the curious coincidence?

I ruminated about product names. What's in a name? Some of the most poorly named products have survived, indeed soared with success. Can there be a more irrelevant name than Arm & Hammer for baking soda? Perhaps the single worst name of all commercially successful products is Chock Full O'Nuts Coffee. Nuts in my coffee? Eghhhh! Yet that product has been one of New York's most successful coffees.

Engelbert Humperdinck? Sambo's? Metamucil? What's in a name? Very little, because any verbal sound can be surrounded with image and aura to give it a special distinction.

The best product name I have ever encountered was created by San Francisco's Doris Craig, who was engaged to name a new suntan lotion that claimed a fast-tanning ingredient. She named it *Tanfastic.* Diagnose that name, if you will. *Tan* describes the function; *fast* describes the claim. And *Tanfastic (Fantastic)* provides the superlative. So how come Tanfastic in the tube went down the tubes altogether?

Could there be an inverse ratio between the relevancy of a product's name and its success in the marketplace? Of course not. But since the relevancy of a name is certainly no guarantee of success, why not simply name the new wine The Argentine Trumpeter and be done with it? Why not indeed! At the very least, it would be expedient, and it would seem unlikely that The Argentine Trumpeter would have been registered, though a check would still be in order.

It was an easy name to sell to the client because the name became a springboard for a legend that I concocted one evening with the help of three martinis:

THE LEGEND OF THE ARGENTINE TRUMPETER

Ornithological texts describe a family of birds called Rails who

> inhabit the vast reaches of the Argentine. Among the Rails, the strangest is the Trumpeter, whose wailing voice and mysterious ways have spawned The Legend Of The Argentine Trumpeter. It is whispered in the vineyards of Mendoza Valley that once she was a grand lady, mourning the loss of her lover. And under her mourning veil was a picture of beautiful tragedy; but also a hint of seduction was reflected in her tearful eyes as she searched the vineyards for another to take her fallen lover's place. But so great was her grief that she leaped from a cliff bordering the river La Plaza. It is said she took wings like a bird and even now wanders the vineyards—half woman, half bird—her tears falling upon the succulent grapes grown for the great wines that bear her name. As you savor this extraordinary wine you will taste a little of this legend; and, it is said that if you are in love and, if you listen with your heart, you will hear the trumpet and cry of this sad and lovely lady—The Argentine Trumpeter.

Hogwash, of course, but surrounded with the right graphics and aura, that "legend" on the back label and "ladybird" pictured on the front label could give the new wine a feeling of integrity and tradition.

Those companies that specialize in product-label design are the fat cats of the advertising/marketing profession. The development and design of a four-inch by six-inch wine label could easily run into six figures. I will share with you a procedure that will enable you to conceptualize and design a powerful and effective new label for a few hundred dollars, plus modest cost of typesetting and finished art.

Much of your initial investment will be in the purchase of all your competitors' products. Here's how Jerry Gibbons and I did it for The Trumpeter. We lined up some twenty bottles of wine, the sample nonlabeled Argentine Trumpeter bottle smack in the middle. To its immediate left we placed a bottle of Paul Masson, a premium California wine, which we presumptuously liked to think would be our principal competitor. To the right was Almaden, another good California wine in the same league. In descending order of competitiveness, other wines, including various California boutique wines and everything from the finest French imports to Annie Greensprings and Ripple made an appearance. We applied considered judgment. For instance, Gallo Hearty Burgundy would be a "closer" competitor to the Argentinian product than a 1967 Chateau Lafite Rothschild. At the two extremes, we placed two distant competitors—on the left, a bottle of imported beer—on the right, a bottle of scotch.

Studying the labels from the middle to right and the middle to left, we started to get a feeling of what would constitute a good label for The Argentine Trumpeter. The most impressive labels and package designs were the non-French imports, those exotic and often disappointing wines from Spain, Hungary, Germany and so on. We concluded at once that restraint would be in order. Embellishments such as mesh wire, hangtags, foil doo-dads and extravagantly whimsical full-color Brueghelesque scenes, while perfectly gorgeous, frequently to the wine aficionado suggest rotgut. But so irresistible were those techniques that we were unwilling to drop them completely.

We kept going back to the tailored and tasteful Paul Masson label. Why not the best of all possible worlds—the pictorial indulgence of the rotgut imports combined with the exquisite design and typographical restraint of Paul Masson? Stealing a man's words is worse than stealing a man's money. But borrowing a man's label can be good business, cost-saving efficiency, and, in fact, the traditional high form of flattery.

The Paul Masson label is printed in classic Roman typeface of which there are some 100 or more different styles. We selected Palatino for The Argentine Trumpeter. Paul Masson's front label features a circular emblem reminiscent of a coat-of-arms. The

Trumpeter label would similarly feature such a device, a cameo shape containing a full-color representation of The Legend of The Argentine Trumpeter. The Paul Masson label is black type on an eggshell ground. The Trumpeter label would be precisely the same coloration.

With blatant disregard for originality and aptness of thought, we swiped the essential ingredients of the Paul Masson label and applied them to The Trumpeter, saving our client a bundle of money and interminable machinations and nitpicking, and ensuring the new product a traditional look of high quality.

Having shamelessly ripped off Paul Masson, we decided we would now upstage Paul Masson by copying the style of Botticelli for the Trumpeter logo. We supplied a fine technician with Botticelli art books and asked that he paint the "legendary" lady in two versions, one for the front label, another for the back label.

The Trumpeter front and back labels and Paul Masson's front label are presented herewith for your inspection, with my special appreciation to Paul Masson, without whose superb graphic taste the Trumpeter label might never have been created.

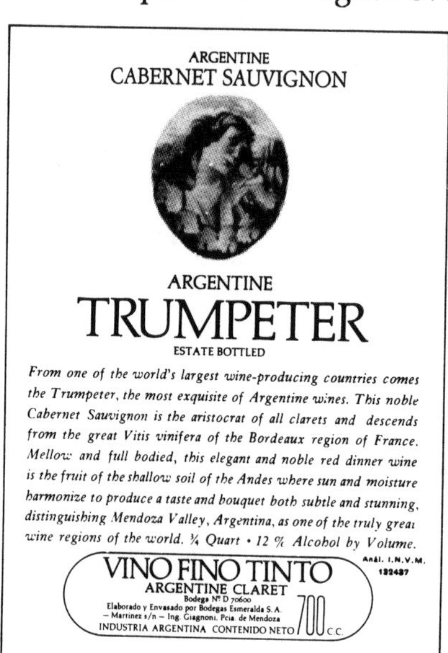

Labels were, of course, in full color.

THE LEGEND OF
THE ARGENTINE TRUMPETER

Ornithological texts describe a family of birds called Rails who inhabit the vast reaches of the Argentine. Among the Rails, the strangest is the Trumpeter, whose wailing voice and mysterious ways have spawned The Legend Of The Argentine Trumpeter. It is whispered in the vineyards of Mendoza Valley that once she was a grand lady, mourning the loss of her lover. And under her mourning veil was a picture of beautiful tragedy; but also a hint of seduction was reflected in her tearful eyes as she searched the vineyards for another to take her fallen lover's place. But so great was her grief that she leaped from a cliff bordering the river La Plata. It is said she took wings like a bird and even now wanders the vineyards – half woman, half bird – her tears falling upon the succulent grapes grown for the great wines that bear her name. As you savor this extraordinary wine you will taste a little of this legend; and, it is said that if you are in love and, if you listen with your heart, you will hear the trumpet and the cry of this sad and lovely lady – the Argentine Trumpeter. ✱ A product of Argentina. Exported by Bodegas Esmeralda S. A. and imported by Scottish & Newcastle Importers Co., San Anselmo, California

CALIFORNIA

BURGUNDY

PAUL MASSON.

RARE PREMIUM WINES

This classic Burgundy comes from superior grape varietals grown to slow maturity in Northern California vineyards. It has a full, deep flavor, a soft texture with a rare bouquet and is a wine of elegant simplicity. This Burgundy should be stored and served at cool cellar temperatures and will render compliments to all main course dishes as well as cheeses. Fine California premium wines since 1852. Made and Bottled by Paul Masson Vineyards, Saratoga, California · Alcohol 12% by Volume.

The architecture of a marketing plan, with its myriad aspects including new product development, advertising campaign, distribution techniques and media considerations, is no less complicated than building a house. Now we had a gorgeous product, but that was only the beginning. Next we would need an advertising campaign and a media budget to underwrite its exposure. Consider, if you will, an advertising campaign slated for full-color, full-page ads to appear in some twenty-three national publications, including *Time, Newsweek, Sports Illustrated, U.S. News & World Report, Fortune, Harper's, Atlantic* and *Forbes.*

Such a campaign would appear to cost in the millions. Not so for The Argentine Trumpeter. For that product the multi-million-dollar *looking* campaign could come in for under five figures.

There was a booming organization headquartered in New York City known to the advertising community as Media Networks, Inc. Through them one could purchase the space for a full-page, full-color ad in *Time, Newsweek, Sports Illustrated* and *U.S. News & World Report* for under $5,885. The catch? The ad would appear only in, let's say, the Beverly Hills editions of those national publications. And while the ad would enjoy the prestige of appearing in a very high quality editorial environment, it would reach only a tiny audience, albeit at an enormous cost per subscriber reached.

This unique media vehicle offers certain advertisers special advantages. A local boutique advertising in a slick national publication a page or two away from DeBeers Diamonds, AT&T or Mercedes-Benz could certainly be judged by readers by the company it keeps. No doubt, certain advertisers promoting new products or services have made an inordinate impression on distributors and retail outlets by promising exposure in the pages of important national magazines—neglecting, of course, to mention that the ad would reach only a geographical pinpoint inhabited by just a handful of prospects.

But The Trumpeter's choice of MNI was motivated by an entirely ethical and practical concern. The Trumpeter introductory test market campaign was limited to forty-four square miles in the San Francisco Bay Area, and MNI's local editions conformed almost exactly to the test market area. Moreover, the thirteen "national" publications that would carry the introductory Trumpeter ad and that would otherwise cost about $17,405 would be provided virtually free, for it developed that Media Networks, Inc. actually *owned* a chunk of Trumpeter wine. Boiled down to its mechanics it worked like this: MNI preprinted the local advertising inserts in increments of four pages. But if the fourth page was not sold to a paying advertiser by the time the deadline for publication and binding had approached, MNI was free to "donate" that page to The Argentine Trumpeter.

I presented the creative work in the New York offices of MNI. Michael Dixon had already seen the label, ads and displays in San Francisco and given the work his blessing. The New York people were equally pleased with the charming campaign featuring the ersatz Legend Of The Argentine Trumpeter and the memorable half-bird, half-lady logo. The program was approved for production and all systems were go. But when I left New York to return home I had disquieting feelings.

In San Francisco, my associate Jerry Gibbons was delighted that our creative strategy had been so gracefully approved—until I dropped the bomb.

"Jerry," I said. "You know we sold those people a very boring campaign?"

"What?" he said. "Boring?" A red mark began to emerge on his forehead, as it frequently did when he was under stress. "Hey, come on, it's a great campaign."

"It's boring—boooooring. Look, didn't we promise Dixon blockbuster ads that would own the magazines? Ads that would get twice, even three times, the readership you usually get with wine ads?"

Jerry agreed, even as the red mark transmuted into purple.

"Well," I said, "we didn't deliver."

We both knew what the other was thinking. All along we had a blockbuster gimmick we had ignored, a device so dramatic and spectacular that if we dared to indulge it, it would overwhelm any magazine in which our ad appeared. The ad could feature the ultimate advertising spokesperson. He could dwarf in sheer drama the Hathaway eyepatch man. Our man was—the one-armed man!

Had we searched 10,000 photo composites at central casting, we could never have found the equal of Michael Dacres Dixon. And he was no mere model, he was the very progenitor of the new wine—charming, distinguished, articulate, aristocratic. And, photographed in a baronial setting, he would elegantly present his wine to the world, his empty right sleeve tucked proudly into his side coat pocket, an empty sleeve that would reach right out and grab the reader.

However, we had already sold another campaign. How now to unsell it? And how, without offending the dear, proud Michael

Dixon, could we persuade him to participate in his own exploitation?

Mr. Michael Dacres Dixon reluctantly submitted—for the good of the company.

The ad *was* a grabber.

It's not long copy that people don't read, it's dull copy. A man interested in purchasing a recreational vehicle will read a thirty-page booklet on RVs. Likewise, wine buffs will not hesitate to read a lengthy, intelligent statement about wine—even in an advertisement. I hope you will savor this copy as did northern Californians when the ad first broke:

Ad appeared in full color.

A SHORT DISCOURSE FROM WINE IMPORTER, MICHAEL DACRES DIXON, ON A MOST PROMISING (PERHAPS EVEN GREAT) NEW WINE.

Introducing The Argentine Trumpeter.

It's no secret that wine from Argentina has never been conspicuous on the world's great wine lists. While some Argentinian wine grapes are of incomparable quality, Argentinian wine in the bottle, historically, has never been suited to the cultivated tastes of wine lovers in the United States and Europe. But now with the introduction of The Argentine Trumpeter, that will all change.

It's a fact that Argentina's Mendoza Valley lies in the very heart of one of the world's two great wine-growing latitudinal belts, where soil and climate harmonize for perfect growing conditions.

It is also a fact that certain grapes grown in Argentina's Mendoza Valley are direct descendants of the great French varietals of Bordeaux.

These simple facts motivated me to travel to Argentina to see what could be done to translate Argentina's superb grapes into an equally superb wine. I think I did it. But the credit must be shared with the tireless Argentinian vintners; and with my traveling companion and adviser, Christopher M. Stevens, who is internationally known as A Master of Europe's Worshipful Company of Vintners.

Priced as low as premium California wines, these limited imports are now available in selected stores in your neighborhood. The wines include Cabernet Sauvignon and Cabernet Malbec.

Should you encounter our new wine, we hope you will trouble to study the label with its Botticelli-like drawings which reveal the haunting story of The Argentine Trumpeter, the half-lady/half-bird, whose tears, according to legend, irrigate the succulent grapes of Mendoza Valley.

We hope The Argentine Trumpeter's rather inelegant price will not in the least deter you from purchasing your first bottle. Thereafter, I am confident you will return time and again to savor the stunning and seductive flavor of the new wine, which we are so pleased and proud to have imported into this country.

MICHAEL DACRES DIXON

When Christ sold his message across the land, he and his disciples could reach only a comparative few. But those few, because they tried his "product" and liked what they got, returned for more. And they told their friends about their satisfactions. And their friends gave it a try and in turn told their friends, and so on. That's the way it worked then, and that's the way it works now.

When we first savored The Argentine Trumpeter we knew it was an extraordinary wine, deserving all the conviction and honest persuasion we could muster. Initial sales to the local northern California trade exceeded 20,000 cases, surpassing Michael Dixon's most optimistic forecasts. The advertising persuaded consumers to try it out, and they loved it and they came back for more and they told their friends.

Unfortunately, soon they stopped telling their friends, because the wine promised was not the wine delivered. While the initial shipment from South America was fine, the successive bulk shipments were hardly comparable to the premium California reds with which we were competing. The wine, it turned out, did not travel well. In the lexicon of the enologist, the wine "bruised." Or was the corking faulty? Did air get in? Whatever happened, it was clear Argentina was not yet the promised land for wine.

Today The Argentine Trumpeter exists only as a parable, a little story to express a truth. This truth is: No product, however effective its advertising, will exist beyond its initial introduction if the advertising promise exceeds the product performance.

⁕

Let me throw a little more water on the subject of print advertising with another reference to Anthony Pools. My first exposure to this giant pool builder was when I was remodeling my home and just after I had been left high and dry by a charlatan pool contractor who went belly up and whose bankruptcy later returned to me $2.56 on my $1,000 deposit check.

I then engaged America's foremost builder of pools, Anthony, who, as it turned out, delivered on all their promises related to quality, budget and construction timetable. So impressed was I by their performance that I called the president of Anthony Pools and offered him my advertising services.

While Anthony was *the* prestige builder of pools, in those days Anthony's advertising was indistinguishable in its graphics and selling thrust from the fly-by-night operators who took your money and ran. Anthony ads were as schlocko as the rest.

An Anthony executive accorded me a courteous telephone reception and informed me that each time they tried to clean up their ads their coupon returns went down. Anthony salesmen were able to close sales on some 35 percent of coupon inquiries. Today, ten little wrinkled coupons torn from a newspaper ad and mailed to Anthony would translate into about $140,000 in gross sales.

Because I was a recent Anthony customer, and notwithstanding my unbridled persistence, Jerry Gibbons and I were granted an audience in the company's South Gate, California headquarters conference room. Jerry came armed with a couple of hundred pool ads torn from the pages of newspapers that circulated in Anthony marketing areas. We wallpapered the walls of the conference room, randomly posting Anthony ads among those of its competitors. Then I produced a stopwatch and gave the Anthony executive staff sixty seconds to find their ads, of which there were many, interspersed among the plethora of shouting, screaming headlines and typographical sameness.

Heads poked forward, brows furrowed, they scanned the walls to find their own ads, but to no avail. Their ads were all but invisible.

"Gentlemen," I announced, "your ads are *just* as invisible in the pages of the Sunday supplements in which you advertise!" Still, they were not persuaded by my theatrics.

The typical pool ad included a "sexy"-looking girl with a bouffant hairdo, propped at the corner of a pool; the "model" was often the daughter or wife of the pool contractor who paid for the ad. The headlines were as tepid as the models were tacky. In one Sunday supplement alone, these pablum headlines appeared:

POOL COUNTRY!

RELIABILITY

HILITE YOUR YARD
(And the pool company was not even called *Hilite.*)

E.O.S. POOL SALE!
(The reader was expected to know that "E.O.S." stood for end-of-season.)

VACATION IN YOUR OWN YARD

PLANNING A POOL?

And there were many more of equal ineptitude.

I implored Anthony to give us a try, maybe just one shot at producing one ad. They could then assess the per-coupon return cost of our advertising effort compared to existing costs. If we could prove that our per-coupon cost was lower on our prototype, premier ad, I suggested that they then retain us for yet a second ad. I assured them that we would depart totally from the industry advertising look, that we would provide high drama, create inordinate impact, express the quality and integrity inherent in the Anthony operation and, most important, reduce the media costs necessary to get coupons returned. They said, "Go," knowing in their hearts that we would flop.

Our ad was four times larger than typical Anthony ads and six times as expensive. It spanned two giant newspaper pages and it contained a second color. But the criterion against which we were working was that of achieving a lower cost per coupon returned. Our ad would have to generate many leads resulting in many increased sales in order to justify its cost. In conceptualizing this test ad, we were equally concerned with formatting a new print campaign for Anthony, so confident were we that its success would guarantee our continued services on their behalf. Accordingly, we thought not just about the single one-shot ad but about the dozens that would have to follow, embracing the same techniques, springing from a common denominator of tone, graphics, typography and psychology which constitute a continuing, cohesive advertising campaign.

While Christ may have been the principal creative genius since the beginning of man, there are others who have shown a similar grand humility combined with good, solid, pragmatic business sense. Certainly, Thomas Edison was among them.

While he "perfected" the light bulb, to the everlasting illumination of mankind, he himself was bright enough to know that it would never sell unless he also perfected a method of mass-producing his invention, funding it and placing it into general distribution. Thus, much of Edison's energy was related to PR-ing his own image, cultivating such admirers as Henry Ford and working out a plan to implement his light bulb invention.

A glass ball that lights up was a fine novelty in the early part of the century. But Edison, like Christ, like Aristotle, like Freud, was interested in so much more than novelty. These men were passionately responding to thunderous inner spirits. They would never be satisfied until they produced results on a very grand scale.

Edison contrived, cajoled, capitulated and almost capsized before he persuaded New York to engage his process to light up Wall Street. He invented not just a light bulb, but a generative, underground system to brighten an entire area—and later an entire planet.

My approach to Anthony was similarly overviewed. I would create not just an interesting novelty ad, but a system of ads, a breakthrough campaign that could go on and on. The campaign would be one that only Anthony, among the hundreds of U.S. pool builders, could use, because it would feature Anthony's single exclusive selling advantage: Anthony is the world's largest builder of pools. From that fact the reader of the ads would be led to deduce reliability, responsibility, quality, economy and permanence. But much more important, the reader would be persuaded by the facts that a commitment to any other pool builder could lead to problems, not the least being the possibility that the builder could go down the drain, leaving the new pool buyer stranded. Indeed, facts revealed that in a ten-year period in California alone, over 200 pool companies either went under or changed their names. Thus, I was, in fact, creating a *fear* campaign.

The opening ad which would determine our future employment by Anthony addressed a tough marketing problem: how to sell swimming pools in the chill of March, when sales are traditionally depressed?

The illustration featured a little man bundled in winter clothing swimming in a kidney-shaped pool from which arose towering icebergs. The headline signaled to the reader that this two-page ad would provide much solid information, not just advertisingese, puffery and empty superlatives:

THE COLD FACTS
ABOUT BUYING A SWIMMING POOL
IN MARCH.

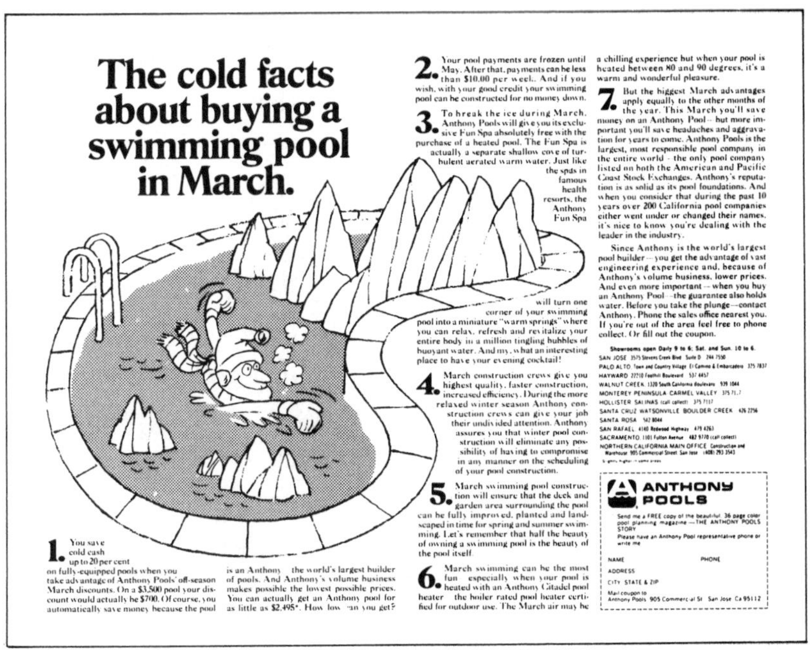

Ad appeared in two colors, black and blue.

The winter ad produced so many coupon leads that the Anthony sales force thought it was summertime. We were engaged to prove our mettle once again with an assignment to create a second ad in the series.

I gave myself the ultimate challenge: create an ad that would dominate the paper, stealing readership from even the hottest news and editorial features. Further, I wanted the ad to command readership not just from immediate prospective pool buyers, but also from an immense market of later-day prospects whose circumstances and income at that time would preclude their even thinking of owning a pool. The ad would also, I decided, be intensely competitive and scrupulously honest. It would persuade the reader that his decision to engage any pool builder other than Anthony would be an invitation to trouble.

To achieve the heroic results I had in mind, the headline would have to be absolute dynamite. Not a single reader would pass the page without being sucked into my ad. That was my intention.

This would be my headline:

**BEST FUCKING POOL
IN THE U.S.A.**

Wow! What a headline! but who would run it? Historically, advertising has been the most timid of all mass communication idioms. In the forties, a meat packer amused the Chicago marketplace with interior bus posters advertising smoked ham: WORTH EVERY HAM CENT. The derring-do of an implied swear word in an ad headline had Chicago commuters, unaccustomed to such license in advertising, smirking all the way to the Loop. While candid language and the most explicit photos have become commonplace in editorial and feature content, advertising has *not* come a long way, baby.

Many issues of *Time* magazine give us a glimpse of bare bosoms and buttocks, but it is always news, never advertising. The July 4, 1978 edition of the *San Francisco Chronicle* carried an AP and UPI news story reporting the obscenity trial of comedian George Carlin. The story printed the seven juciest expletives in the English language. Most of the same words appeared in the syndicated television masterpiece, *Scared Straight,* which was broadcast into millions of homes during high viewing hours. In *Playboy* magazine, which reaches over 9,000,000 adult readers, there is no recess or appendage this prestigious vehicle for national advertising has not displayed in naked living color—opposite ads or only a page away from ads for Gillette, Firestone, General Motors and the U.S. Navy. But even in that permissive environment, the advertisers stay buttoned down, bottled up and boring.

It used to be the habit of the *New Yorker* magazine to airbrush the crotches of male models if there was even a hint in the ads of anatomy in that forbidden area. Have things loosened up since? Maybe a little, but in no way compared to changes in the editorial area. Case in point: I once shared an evening of elegant dining with a *Playgirl* magazine editor. "In the next issue," she explained in her executive, corporate voice, "we're showing erections. We think the readers are ready for it."

"But are the advertisers?" I asked.

"Of course not," she said. "But we won't lose any."

I have always been astounded at the Puritan lament that there is too much sex in advertising. Too little, I say.

BEST FUCKING POOL IN THE U.S.A. Of course, that headline would never fly. The client would never buy it, the consumer would never accept it, the papers would never run it and I would certainly never recommend it. While the consuming public is tolerant and permissive about news and entertainment, it has been conditioned by the advertisers themselves, with some recent exceptions in the fashion and cosmetic industries, (thank you, Calvin Klein) to expect conservative good taste in advertising.

This exercise in thought-meandering is not meant to lead to the conclusion that advertising can or should be as bold and candid as the news, editorial and entertainment content of our mass media. It is meant only to highlight the spectrum of boring to bold and to encourage advertisers to at least recognize the permissive environments in which their advertising often appears so that they may feel comfortable in being a lot less fearful and a little more daring.

I would, of course, modify my Anthony headline. It would be as sexy as any "respectable" ad could be and yet it would be bolder than any pool ad had ever been before. The Anthony headline that would break the bank was:

A WORD ABOUT NUDE SWIMMING

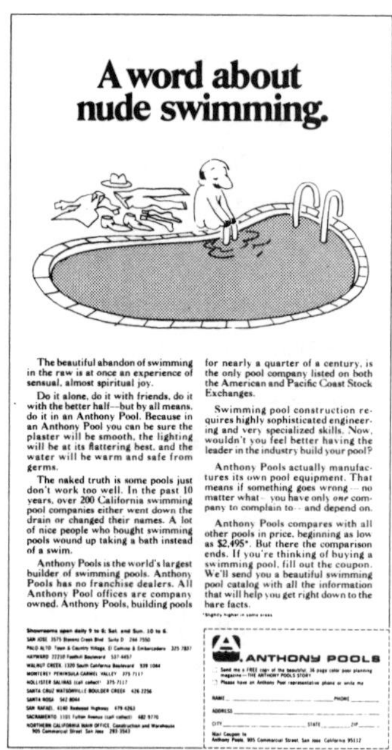

Ad appeared in two colors, black and blue

As you study the text of this ad, I trust you will concur that the headline is relevant, that the facts are persuasive and that I succeeded in building doubts, fears even, in the minds of potential pool buyers should they risk purchasing a pool other than one built by Anthony.

A WORD ABOUT
NUDE SWIMMING

The beautiful abandon of swimming in the raw is at once an experience of sensual, almost spiritual joy.

Do it alone, do it with friends, do it with the better half—but by all means, do it in an Anthony Pool. Because in an Anthony Pool you can be sure the plaster will be smooth, the lighting will be at its flattering best, and the water will be warm and safe from germs.

The naked truth is some pools just don't work too well. In the past 10 years, over 200 California swimming pool companies went down the drain or changed their names. A lot of nice people who bought swimming pools wound up taking a bath instead of a swim.

Anthony Pools is the world's largest builder of swimming pools. Anthony Pools has no franchise dealers. All Anthony Pool offices are company owned. Anthony Pools, building pools for nearly a quarter of a century, is the only pool company listed on both the American and Pacific Coast Stock Exchanges.

Swimming pool construction requires highly sophisticated engineering and very specialized skills. Now, wouldn't you feel better having the leader in the industry build your pool?

Anthony Pools actually manufactures its own pool equipment. That means if something goes wrong—no matter what—you have only *one* company to complain to—and depend upon.

Anthony Pools compares with all other pools in price. But there the comparison ends. If you're thinking of buying a swimming pool, fill out the coupon. We'll send you a beautiful swimming pool catalog with all the information that will help you get right down to the bare facts.

ANTHONY POOLS

The Anthony ads reproduced below illustrate the continuity of design and concept which characterized the entire series.

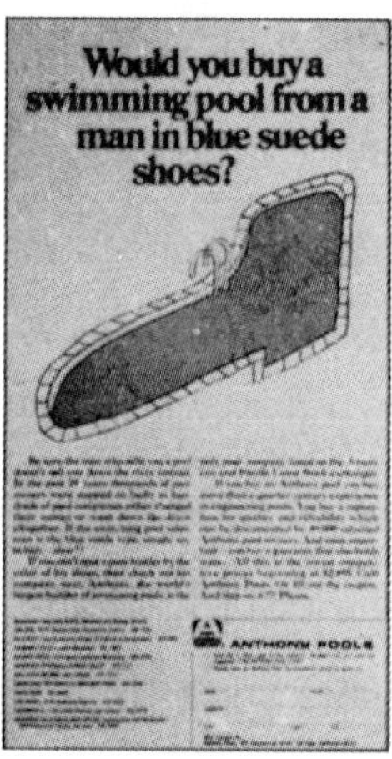

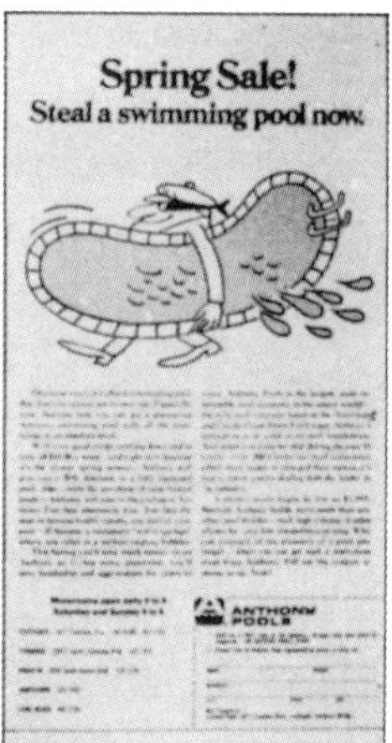

Ad appeared in two colors, black and blue.

The great copywriters and advertising artists do not write words and draw pictures. They write and draw ideas. Given a few educated skills, the truly great ideas will write and design themselves. Do not search for words, search for ideas—and when you find the big idea, the words will almost write themselves.

Suppose you were advertising for a grocery chain with a special on eggs, 79 cents a dozen. You have a million words to choose from. Pick a few and express that product special with a drama as high as the price is low. Think for a moment: What would you say to grab the attention and make the sale?

Suppose this advertising assignment were given to Mark Twain or Hemingway or Aristotle or Christ himself. Whatever would they write to express this simple idea, this unprecedented value?

You know what they would write:

EGGS, 79¢ A DOZEN

Great advertising, great anything, pure and simple, is—pure and simple.

CHAPTER XI

"CHRONICLES" WISDOM AND WEALTH FOR THE RETAILERS

In Second Chronicles of the Old Testament, God speaks to Solomon: "Knowledge is granted unto thee; and I will give thee riches and wealth."

In today's Chronicles—The San Francisco Chronicle, The Houston Chronicle, The Muskegan Chronicle, the Spokane Chronicle, the Green Bay Chronicle and morning and evening Chronicles throughout the U.S., retailers can dip into riches and wealth worth more than 4 billion dollars. By applying some rarely used techniques, they can cut their newspaper advertising budgets by 25% or more and even increase their ad's readership at the same time.

Most retailers are the little guys in advertising who can least afford to waste even a nickle in non-productive advertising. The retailer's traditional support and all too often crutch is the daily newspaper.

The retailers are the shops and services in your community—the downtown piano store, the neighborhood savings and loan, the video rental outlet, the small haberdashery chain, the automobile dealership, the optometrist, the office equipment store, the aerobics salon, the community repertory theater, the steak restaurant, the kitchen/bath remodeling people, the hair transplant place—all those big and little shops and services who spend more than they should on advertising, rarely see any direct results from their advertising investments and are terrified to cut back their advertising budgets lest business becomes worse than it already is.

While the small business and service entrepreneurs underwrite the larger number of retail newspaper ads, the greatest dollar volume comes from the local department stores and large local clothiers, some of whom, in the urban centers, spend more than 5 million a year in a single local newspaper.

Not counting the national ads (i.e. tobacco, booze, automotive, etc.) and the classified ads, daily and afternoon newspapers gobble 16 billion local advertising dollars a year. My own conservative estimate is that 25% of that cost can be cut, at no loss to the consumer sales, by reducing the size of the ads, re-tailoring the layouts, re-designing the typography and re-thinking the contents of the ads. At the same time retailers are saving 4 billion dollars they can add a bonus impact and increased readership. This chapter will tell you how to do it.

First, some basic smarts about newspaper advertising. Newspapers are a NEWS medium. If you do not have something new or newsworthy to say about your product or service you should not be advertising in newspapers. It is simply too expensive a medium to be used for reminder advertising.

A shoppers special or sale price for goods or services is news and newspapers are the perfect medium to deal with sales. A higher interest rate on T bills or a lower interest rate on mortgage loans is news. The grand opening of a restaurant is news and so is a display ad announcing that the Beijing Circus is coming to town.

Mon., August 9, 19.. San Francisco Chronicle 17

THE BRIDGE COLUMN

CHARLES H. GOREN AND OMAR SHARIF

The bidding:

South	West	North	East
2 ♠	Pass	4 ♠	Pass
Pass	Pass		

Opening lead: Jack of

West led the jack of hearts. East won the ace and returned the three. Declarer played low; East won the 10 and continued with the king. After ruffing the heart in dummy, declarer drew trumps in three rounds, then cashed the ace-king of diamonds. He now tried to reach dummy by leading a club to the queen.

East won the king and returned a heart. Declarer ruffed, but since he had no way to get to dummy to use his good diamonds, he had to concede another club for down one.

The fates were not kind to declarer. He would have romped home had either trumps split evenly or had the king of clubs been with West. Or, for that matter, if he had played the hand a bit better.

See the difference if declarer refuses to ruff the third heart in dummy, discarding a club instead and letting West hold the trick. If West returns a minor suit, declarer wins, draws three rounds of trumps and unblocks the diamonds. Now he can enter dummy with a trump and take two discards on dummy's good diamonds.

Actually, West's best defense is to play a fourth heart. But declarer can counter by discarding another club from dummy and ruffing in his hand. He can then reach dummy with a club ruff.

CHESS

GEORGE KOLTANOWSKI

White to play and mate in three moves.

The U.S. Junior Open Champion-

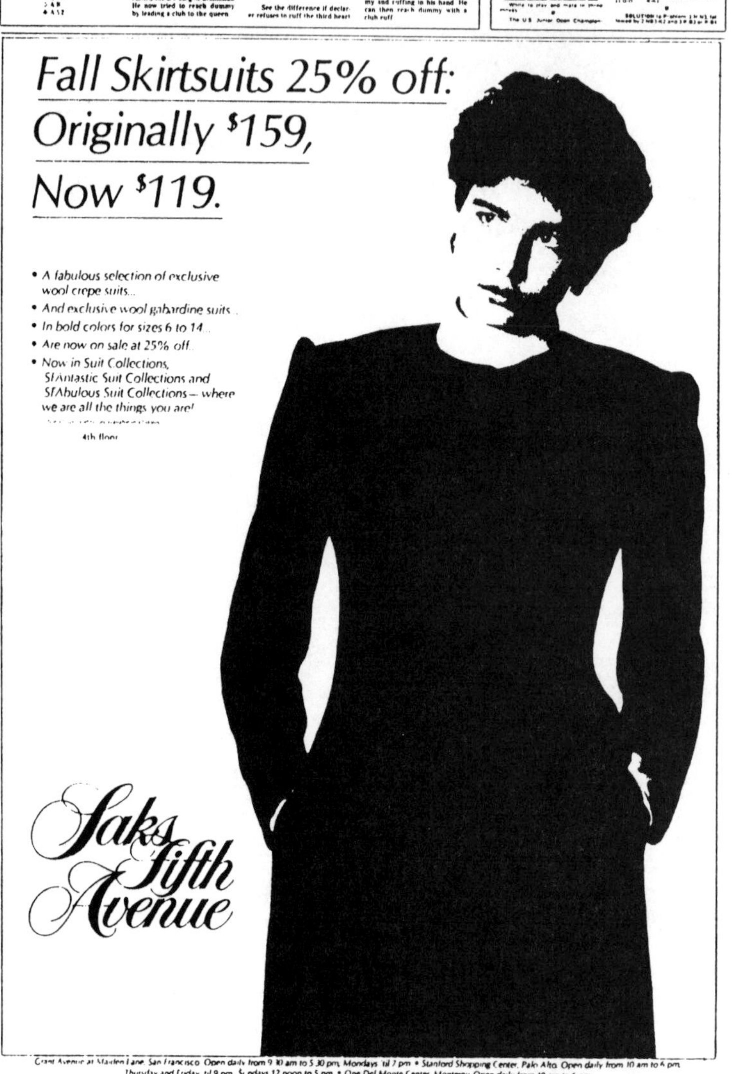

While we will be talking about Saks Fifth Avenue for the next number of pages please understand that this exercise could just as easily be about Tiny Tots Diaper Service, Lydia's Flower Store, Golden Oaks hardwood Floors, Sears Rent A Car, MidTown Fabrics, anyone who may take display space in a newspaper.

Today the Saks newspaper ad on the left page, scaled-down to accommodate the parameters of a book page, would cost Saks $14, 538 for a single display for one day only in the San Francisco Chronicle. In the lexicon of the ad man it is called a "scotch page" because it is just short of being a full page. Saks showed good judgment in opting to share the page with the bridge and puzzle people Goren and Koltonowski because if purchased as additional advertising space, the top three inches of this page (actually 18 column inches) would have cost Saks an additional $2029 but would not have delivered a single additional reader for the Saks ad. Indeed, the very fact that chess and crossword aficionados may have read the top of the page gave Saks an advantage. How many thousands of eyes were trapped on that page because of the Goren/Koltonowski attraction. How many of those eyes, that would otherwise have been blind to the Saks ad, dropped downward a few inches to discover the skirtsuit sale at 25% off.

Beware of the full-page newspaper ad. Sometimes there is actually an inverse ration between the size of an ad and the size of the readership it achieves. Good going Saks—but go a little further next time. Turn the page you'll see what I mean.

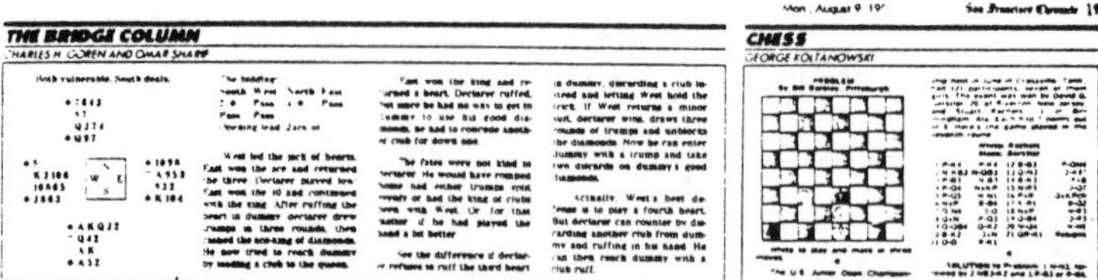

Mon., August 9, 19[illegible] San Francisco Chronicle 19

THE BRIDGE COLUMN

CHARLES H. GOREN AND OMAR SHARIF

Both vulnerable. South deals.

The bidding:

South	West	North	East
1 ♠	Pass	4 ♠	Pass
Pass	Pass		

Opening lead: Jack of ♥

West led the jack of hearts. East won the ace and returned the three. Declarer played low. East won the 10 and continued with the king. After ruffing the heart in dummy, declarer drew trumps in three rounds, then cashed the ace-king of diamonds. He now tried to reach dummy by leading a club to the queen.

East won the king and returned a heart. Declarer ruffed, but since he had no way to get to dummy to use his good diamonds, he had to concede another club for down one.

The fates were not kind to declarer. He would have romped home had either trumps split evenly or had the king of clubs been with West. Or for that matter if he had played the hand a bit better.

See the difference if declarer refuses to ruff the third heart in dummy, discarding a club instead and letting West hold the trick. If West returns a minor suit, declarer wins, draws three rounds of trumps and unblocks the diamonds. Now he can enter dummy with a trump and take two discards on dummy's good diamonds.

Actually, West's best defense is to play a fourth heart. But declarer can counter by discarding another club from dummy and ruffing in his hand. He can then reach dummy with a club ruff.

CHESS

GEORGE KOLTANOWSKI

War Plot to Drop Diseased Rats From Balloons

San Francisco Chronicle 11 ★ Mon., August 9, 1982

Tokyo

In a deathbed confession, a former Japanese army doctor disclosed a bizarre World War II plot to spread pestilence in the United States by using rat-laden balloons, a Japanese news agency reported yesterday.

Kyodo News Service said the physician, whose identity was withheld, disclosed the plot before his death in late January in a confession to a Catholic missionary friend.

The physician, who until his death at the age of 71 ran a clinic in Kobe province, south of Tokyo, was quoted as saying "I was engaged in a medical science designed to kill people.

"The peace we have today is very valuable and we should never have war again."

He said he wanted his confession to contribute to historical knowledge, Kyodo reported.

Kyodo said the project in which the physician was engaged called for launching balloons carrying rats and plague-spreading fleas contained in ceramic pods.

The report comes amid angry protest from China that revisions to Japan's standard high school history books whitewash atrocities Japan committed before and during World War II.

You think this is the same ad, don't you? Wrong. Take another look. This ad has been shrunk top to bottom, by an additional two inches of the newspaper page. Net savings for one day's exposure is an additional $1,352. Flip this page back and forth with the previous page. For all substantive reasons this ad is identical to the other. Yet, this smaller ad has an advantage over the previous ad. Even though it is smaller it will likely get more readership because now it is sharing the page with WAR PLOT TO DROP DISEASED RATS FROM BALLOONS. Perhaps the readers' eyes will also drop—down a few inches to the skirtsuit ad, thus giving Saks some bonus readers.

Whether your retail store is pushing ties, toys, tires, trousers or tattoos, the main purpose of your ad is to dispense information about your product. Slicing two inches from the Saks ad did not sacrifice a smidgen of information. Most products are bilaterally symmetrical so if you show one side you have shown the other. Whether you are designing a tire ad or a trouser ad, keep in mind that you don't have to display the entire item. You may count on the reader to conclude that a pant leg drops all the way down to the shoe and that a section of a tire has the same tread characteristics as the entire circumference. Crop the photo, shrink the ad, trim the budget. Imagine the big bucks Saks could have saved. But there's even more to be saved. Turn page, please...

U.S. Reportedly Plans to Sell Even More Weapons Abroad

Washington

The United States, having begun to increase military aid and arms sales abroad, is planning to expand them steadily through 1984 and beyond in an effort to gain political influence and access to foreign bases, according to senior officials.

Italy Awaits Talks for New Government

British General Warns Argentina

Some department store or clothier advertisers who purchase large display space will argue that if they shrink their ads they may lose what they regard as preferred placement up front in the main news section of the daily newspaper. Actually, their up-front ads may be in a disadvantageous position competing for readership with the hard news headlines rather than the softer news headlines deeper into the paper. If you sacrifice your front position because you have shrunk your ad maybe you have actually gained an advantage.

The incredible shrinking ad is now less than sixty percent its original size. But note that it still dominates the page; not a single word of copy has been deleted and the typography is the same point size as the original ad. But now, the little lady with the dazed look is even more interesting because she is in the company of a British General, an Italian President and a guy who just had a hair transplant. She still owns the page and nobody gives a hoot, a string of beans or a rat's you-know-what that her left sleeve has been cropped.

Had the Saks people shrunk their original ads to this size they would have saved more than $5,156 for the single insertion or more than 35% the cost of the ad space. Were Saks to apply this technique to their entire budget for newspaper space in Northern California they would save over a million clams every year.

What if Saks were to come down to an even smaller size? Would it be a come-down for Saks? Do you lose prestige when you lose column inches? Of course not. While Saks is saving you 25% on their skirtsuit sale they could have saved themselves over 70% on their ad. Flip page please.

'Dust Bowl' Home

'The Dust Bowl of Wilmington' is what these four transients call their two makeshift tents in Los Angeles. Sharon Royce (left), Andrew Williams, Donald Daniels, Mark — he would not tell his last name — and another male live near rats and garbage. They say they have nowhere else to go, and they refuse to accept welfare.

Mandatory Prison Doesn't Cut Crime, Study Reports

Washington

Mandatory prison terms for lawbreakers do not necessarily reduce crime, according to a new study prepared for the Justice Department.

In the study, released yesterday, researchers examined New York's required imprisonment of certain drug offenders and a Massachusetts law mandating a one-year prison term for illegal possession of a gun.

"Although the intent has been to reduce crime by increasing the certainty and severity of punishment, the available evidence shows a large gap between legislative intent and actual criminal justice practice," the report said.

"It is difficult, perhaps impossible, to substantiate the claim that mandatory sentencing is an effective tool for reducing crime," it said.

The report, prepared by a private consulting firm for the department's National Institute of Justice, does not necessarily reflect the department's views.

Thirty-two states have mandatory sentences, many of them for gun-related crimes, according to the American Civil Liberties Union.

The consulting firm, Abt Associates Inc. of Cambridge, Mass., noted that following enactment of sentencing laws, drug deaths in New York City fell, and armed assault, armed robbery and homicides dipped in Massachusetts.

Associated Press

A Controversy Rages

Crime's Link to Hard Times

Washington

The last time unemployment rates were this high, in the Great Depression, John Dillinger was making withdrawals from banks along with Ma Barker and Bonnie and Clyde.

It might seem that in the current recession, as waves of marginal workers and others lose their jobs, more crime is inevitable. But an analysis of crime data and unemployment rates for the last 30 years shows no strong relationship.

Some experts say recessions mean escalating crime; others argue that there is no evidence to link rising unemployment with rising crime. The problem is that crime statistics are notoriously unreliable, partly because only a fraction of crimes committed are reported to authorities.

Looking at nationwide crime statistics in seven categories — auto theft, burglary, robbery, property crime, other larceny, violent crime and overall crimes committed — and using various statistical methods, the Washington Post compared the incidence of crime in the seven categories with nationwide unemployment rates from 1960 through 1981.

In the recession year of 1975, when unemployment reached 8.5 percent, the total crime index reached a peak with historic highs in violent crime, robbery, burglary and auto theft.

Some of those peaks were reached again in 1979 and 1980 as the crime rate crept up again after dropping when the 1975 recession ended. In general, both the crime and the unemployment rates have tended to rise since 1970.

On the other hand, 1961 was also a year of high unemployment although by today's standards the 6.7 percent rate seems low. Yet in that year there were drops in violent crime, murder, rape, robbery and aggravated assault. Furthermore, while the unemployment rate declined from 1961 to 1969 the crime rate rose substantially.

The analyses show only a slight relationship between crime and unemployment. When unemployment rises it is likely that most types of crime will rise only a little more than they would otherwise.

The question of the unemployment-crime relationship, if any, has consumed much ink and computer time in the academic world. M. Harvey Brenner, a sociologist at Johns Hopkins University in Baltimore, has published controversial findings that there is a link between unemployment and many crimes, particularly murder.

Brenner says he believes a 1 percent increase in the unemployment rate is associated with a 5.7 percent rise in murders and a 4 percent increase in the number of people in state prisons. He also reports that each 1 percent rise in unemployment is tied to a 4.1 percent increase in suicide, a 1.9 percent rise in the overall mortality rate and increases of 4.3 percent among men and 2.3 percent among women newly admitted to mental hospitals.

While Brenner stands by these figures six years after he presented them to a congressional committee, he cautions that a recession does not automatically mean more crime. He believes it is safest to say that all things being equal, more unemployment will result in higher crime rates.

Brenner says the most important aspect of unemployment is joblessness among males aged 15 to 24. If the ratio of unemployed young males to all unemployed people rises, then he said increases in crime are particularly likely. Many types of crimes, even rape, are affected, he said.

A principal reason for this relationship, according to Brenner, is stress. When people are out of work, they feel tension. They may also feel victimized, and there may be economic reasons for committing thefts or burglaries, so some of their number turn to crime.

He emphasizes that there are many other causes of crime: increasing use of alcohol and narcotics, urban growth, development of an "underclass" and demographic and family changes.

Other scholars have roundly criticized Brenner's work and have reached different conclusions from the same data. The statistical analysis is extremely complex because the data are not always reliable and comparable, and because there are many factors to be taken into account.

Frederick C. Nold, president of a research company in Palo Alto, worked with some of Brenner's data and found different results. In particular, Nold said the most important factor is the proportion of young males in the unemployment figures. The overall rate of unemployment is much less important, Nold said.

"It doesn't demonstrate much of a relationship between crime and (overall) unemployment," he said.

Harvard Professor James Q. Wilson, an authority on crime, criticized Brenner's work and said, "Overall unemployment seems to bear little or no relationship to crime."

Reliable national data are not available for the Depression years, Wilson said, adding that a review he conducted of local studies on unemployment and crime found no overall relationship.

"There's no basis for a prediction that a deepening or continuing of the recession will lead to increases in the crime rate," Wilson said.

Washington Post

Murder Charge

Vandergrift, Pa.

A 21-year-old man has been charged with killing his grandparents whose bodies were found nine days after they were reported to have left their home unlocked and with fresh apple dumplings left out, [illegible] authorities said. Robert [illegible] of Greensburg was charged Saturday night with two counts of criminal homicide. He was being held in lieu of $100,000 bond.

Associated Press

Members Only

Exclusive Timeshare Ownership on Nob Hill Forever

Powell Place

[illegible]

Powell Place

An Uncommon Offer, Regrettably Limited

LEARN HOW TO RESHAPE AN ORGANIZATION

A MASTERS FROM USF CAN IMPROVE YOUR ORGANIZATIONAL EFFECTIVENESS

Now you can earn a Masters in Human Relations and Organization Development from USF in as little as 18 months...without quitting your present job. It's an intensive program especially designed to provide working professionals with skills for understanding the issues and problems facing today's organizations.

You'll meet once a week with a small group of fellow professionals to learn techniques and strategies for improving organizational effectiveness. You'll become expert in applying the problem solving skills that are necessary in today's rapidly-changing environment.

Classes are forming now. So do something smart. If you're even the least bit interested, call today for full information.

CALL 415-666-6656

USF
University of San Francisco

The Chronicle ad which Saks ran in the daily cost them $12,510 and spanned 240 square inches. This miniaturized lets-pretend version of the same ad is only 70 square inches—less than a third the original size and the Chronicle would have sold Saks the space for $3,381. The type, while modestly smaller than the original is surely more readable, more in scale with the editorial headlines and the editorial copy, which are the reasons people purchased the newspaper in the first place. Note the heavy black border around the Saks ad. This gives the ad increased presence on the page and prevents the ad from melting into the adjacent ads.

If clothier and department store advertisers purchasing large display space reduced their ads by fifty percent or more—they would surely not lose readership in the same proportion that they would be saving money. Huge, outsized ads are incompatible with the environment of a newspaper and often will discourage readership by their very blatant and aggressive presence. Four inch letters screaming SALE one foot from my face may look good on a layout man's drawing board—but it's a turn-off in the daily newspaper.

WE'LL TREAT YOU WITH RESPECT, CONCERN AND UNDERSTANDING.

BUT DON'T WORRY, YOU'LL GET USED TO IT.

Let's face it. When it comes to respect, concern and understanding, most people rank banks right up there with the phone company and the Internal Revenue Service.

So if you're a little skeptical when you see these words in a bank ad, well, we understand.

All we ask is a chance to prove to you that, at 1st Nationwide Bank, they're more than just words.

They're the philosophy which has helped us grow from a tiny savings and loan to a full service financial institution with branches in 12 states and over $15 billion in assets. And you'll see this philosophy reflected in everything we do.

Take the new branches we've been opening inside select K mart stores. These conveniently located branches offer our customers longer hours, ample parking and all the great service they've become accustomed to.

If you'd like to check us out for yourself, we invite you to stop by any 1st Nationwide Bank. Or call us toll free at (800) 245-0111.

1ST NATIONWIDE BANK
A FEDERAL SAVINGS BANK

1ST NATIONWIDE NETWORK

FSLIC

The average reader will hold a book approximately ten inches from the tip of his nose, as you are probably doing now. Look at the 1ST NATIONWIDE BANK ad on the left page and pull the book toward you until your nose touches the T in the middle of the the word UNDERSTANDING.

While respect, concern and understanding is a very good advertising concept for a financial institution, it is clear that the designer of this full page newspaper ad is not understanding some simple basics about readability. Just as the headline words blurred as your nose touched the page—so did the headline blur in the pages of the newspapers that this ad ran. In the actual ad each character is 1 1/2 inch high. Reading the newspaper page at ten inches from ones nose—produces a jangle of typographic confusion necessitating that the reader, assuming his interest is engaged in the first place, read the outsized heading at arms length. If 1ST NATIONWIDE BANK really wanted to treat its prospective depositors with RESPECT, CONCERN AND UNDERSTANDING—they would be well advised to start out by designing an ad that expresses those virtues. Consumer, beware of big hype; advertiser, beware of BIG TYPE.

Gravity Will Assist

Galileo's Roundabout Mission Plans

By Warren E. Leary
New York Times

New York

The Galileo space probe on Thursday is to begin a looping, circuitous waltz across the heavens during which it will change planetary partners three times and make fleeting passes by other bodies on its journey to Jupiter.

The countdown began yesterday for the launching aboard the space shuttle Atlantis, which will carry the three-ton robot spacecraft into Earth orbit. From there, a booster rocket will send it on its mission to Jupiter by first firing it in the opposite direction.

The mission will make the most extensive use to date of the gravitational fields of other planets and moons to accelerate and maneuver a craft through space.

The National Aeronautics and Space Administration was driven to this ingenious and complicated plan in the aftermath of the Challenger disaster because it had failed to provide a sufficiently safe and powerful rocket to boost Galileo to Jupiter directly.

Gravity Assists

The circuitous route will allow the spacecraft to pick up enough speed from gravity assists to reach the giant planet, but the trip will take six years instead of the originally planned 2½ years and will cost far more than originally estimated.

In its roundabout trek to Jupiter, Galileo will first fly to Venus before looping back to the Earth. It will pass within 600 miles of its home planet, and use gravity for a kick that will send it out as far as the asteroid belt between Earth and Mars.

This elongated orbit will bring it back to Earth a second time, where it will make a startlingly close pass of 185 miles above the surface, a bit less than the distance from New York City to Harrisburg, Pa. As it passes, it will pick up [illegible] miles an hour of additional speed, enough to shoot it outbound toward Jupiter.

"Without question, this is the most complicated gravity assist mission so far," said Dr. William J. O'Neil of the National Aeronautics and Space Administration's Jet Propulsion Laboratory, which is in charge of the mission. "It is intricate and ambitious, but we are very confident about it."

Detailed Look

The Galileo mission will be the first to orbit and study one of the giant outer planets in detail rather than just speed by for a cursory look.

The large craft, bristling with instruments, signals a new era of gathering the subtle, long-term data necessary for comprehensive understanding of a planet.

The gravity assist technique allows a spacecraft to gain energy by being pulled toward a planet or moon at ever-increasing speed then use that speed to break loose from the larger body's gravity after swinging around it, and to depart at much higher speed and in a different direction.

By United Press International

Shuttle commander Donald Williams waved to reporters as crew members Michael McCulley (left) and Shannon Lucid watched

The technique, pioneered by American engineers and scientists has become essential to interplanetary exploration, experts said.

"All of the major outer-planet missions for the balance of this century and into the next would not be possible without using gravitational assist," said O'Neil, the science and mission design manager for Galileo.

Voyager 2 Mission

The recently completed Voyager 2 mission to the outer planets involved successively using the gravity of Jupiter, Saturn, Uranus and Neptune to fling the craft onward to new targets.

Although Voyager's gravity assists were by no means simple, engineers note that the craft's course was a rather straightforward one aimed at objects lying in the same general direction.

Galileo, on the other hand, will require tricky maneuvers at both ends of its six-year trip to Jupiter, dashing and swinging around numerous bodies to achieve its many goals.

Scientists and engineers said Galileo, named after the 17th century Italian scientist who discovered Jupiter's four major moons with one of the first telescopes, will be the most advanced interplanetary spacecraft ever launched and the first to orbit one of the giant outer planets.

Jupiter's Moons

The principal aim of the project, which has already cost more than $1.4 billion, is to make the most extensive study yet of Jupiter and its 16 moons, including launching a probe into the giant planet's turbulent atmosphere for the first time.

The Jovian system is considered in many ways to be a miniature model of the solar system, and scientists hope to learn more about planetary formation and evolution by studying it.

In addition, the nuclear-powered spacecraft crammed with 15 scientific instruments has lesser missions, like making the first close-up visits to two asteroids, briefly surveying Venus and Earth

> *'It is intricate and ambitious, but we are very confident about it'*

and examining the dark side of Earth's moon.

Five months before reaching Jupiter, Galileo is to release a 744-pound probe that will take a course of its own to the gaseous planet. The cone-shaped device will plunge into the atmosphere at 115,000 miles per hour and will slow to a few hundred miles an hour behind a searing, 28,000-degree Fahrenheit shock wave.

Once slowed, the probe will eject its heat shields, open a parachute and float about 125 miles down into Jupiter's clouds before atmospheric pressure crushes it.

75 Minutes

During its expected 75-minute life in the planet's atmosphere, which is composed mostly of light gases such as hydrogen and helium, the probe will send data about the composition of the atmosphere to the Galileo orbiter for relay back to Earth.

After going into orbit around Jupiter with a gravity assist from the volcanic moon Io, Galileo will spend 22 months studying the planet and its moons while making 10 long, looping orbits through the system and will perform still more gravitational gymnastics.

Each time the spacecraft comes near one of the four major moons, it is to make a close, gravity-assisted pass that will change its orbit and bring it closer to other moons.

One of the most spectacular examples of using gravity assist in the inner solar system occurred in 1983 when scientists figured out a way to hijack an old satellite that was parked between the Earth and the sun to study solar wind and make it the first spacecraft to probe a comet.

U.S. Left Out

A fleet of five spacecraft from Europe, Japan and the Soviet Union was to fly by Halley's comet in 1986, but because of budgetary and planning problems, the United States was the only space power that did not have a mission planned for the famed comet's visit, which occurs only once every 75 years.

But the United States, using some precise calculations and help from the moon's gravity, upstaged other nations a bit by becoming the first to visit a comet.

Dr. Robert Farquhar of NASA's Goddard Space Flight Center and the late Dr. Fred Scarf of TRW Inc. figured out a way to maneuver the International Sun-Earth Explorer 3 spacecraft so that it eventually intercepted and flew through the tail of comet Giacobini-Zinner on Sept. 11, 1985.

The feat required 37 rocket firings and five swings around the moon, the last a harrowing speed run Dec. 22, 1983, that took the craft within 75 miles of the lunar surface before flinging it off to its comet rendezvous.

"When you have many, many swing-bys on the same mission, that's when you get creative," said Farquhar.

Child-Care Bills Near Completion

New York Times

Washington

Federal legislation that vastly expands the federal government's role in providing child care assistance is nearing completion in Congress.

Supporters of the legislation predict that they will overcome any remaining obstacles, including the threat of a presidential veto.

The congressional push for passage puts President Bush in an awkward political position. Although he supported child-care assistance in last year's presidential campaign, he has raised both budgetary and ideological concerns about various bills now before Congress.

Bush had originally proposed legislation that would cost an estimated $2.5 billion a year by 1993 through an income tax credit for lower income families.

Bush's proposal did not call for direct spending for day-care centers. It did contain a $250 million increase in spending for the Head Start program, an education program for preschool children.

The more expensive Democratic plans, estimated to cost from $10.3 billion to $22 billion over five years, call for expanding tax credits and also propose grants to the states to provide money for direct assistance for child care.

A House plan to expand tax credits alone, which was sponsored by Representative Mickey Edwards, R-Okla., and backed by Bush, failed last week on a 205-to-140 vote in the House.

A plan supported by the administration was previously rejected by the Senate, prompting Marlin Fitzwater, presidential spokesman, to declare the Senate-approved plan a veto candidate, but stopped short of saying the president would actually reject the legislation.

The legislation awaits a House and Senate conference committee that will reconcile differences in two Democratic versions of the bill passed by the House last week with a measure adopted by the Senate in June.

Meetings between the two houses [illegible] held up by the Senate's [illegible] capital gains [illegible].

The measures approved in both the House and Senate [illegible] tax credit [illegible] increased grants to the states for child care.

The measures leave the White House in the position of threatening a veto of family oriented legislation that received powerful encouragement in July 1988 when Bush, then his party's expected presidential nominee, endorsed tax credits for child care as policy that illustrated the compassionate side of his presidency. Bush was also seeking to attract the support of women voters.

Representative Thomas Downey of New York, a Democratic manager of the House bill, said yesterday that House and Senate negotiators faced a daunting challenge on reaching a compromise on complex and competing concepts, including the magnitude of assistance, the size of the tax credit and ways to provide funds to the states.

However, representatives of child-care advocacy groups said the legislation the House and Senate could be reconciled because they [illegible] goals.

Both bills would help low income families pay the cost of care, so they can be sure their kids are getting safe and decent care," said Mary Poundstone, spokeswoman for the Children's Defense Fund.

Each year newspaper advertisers spend billions of dollars on newspaper space and then neglect to apply printers ink to the space that they have purchased. A parallel in broadcast would be to purchase radio time and neglect to provide sound or to purchase television time and neglect to provide a picture.

The phenomenon known as whitespace has mesmerized art directors and advertising layout people for decades. The presumption that nothingness or whitespace is and of itself a commanding and riveting attraction is hogwash. The space cadet whitespace ad designers who win awards in graphic competitions are costing their clients dearly.

The costly, $4,170 one-third page newspaper ad on the left is a lovely example of whitespace lunacy. Since many people read their daily newspaper folded, first above the fold then below the fold—they would never have an opportunity to even know what this ad was trying to express. Note the subhead at the bottom of the ad, OUR RATE IS WAY UP THERE. You bet it is, baby—especially for the cost of that ad.

Now redwoods aren't the only trees people look for in Northern California.

When in Sausalito, we invite you to look for the new Timberland Store at 668 Bridgeway. A store where you'll find the world's finest collection of footwear, apparel and accessories for men and women. Including handsewn boat shoes and seaworthy marine gear. Hand-knit sweaters. Shearling coats. And premium leather boots. Outdoor clothing so deeply rooted in a tradition of craftsmanship, it promises to take its place among the Bay Area's most enduring attractions.

The Timberland Store

I am wasting yet another page in my book to dramatize the waste of whitespace.

After glancing at the headline on the left page newspaper ad—I wondered what other kind of trees people were looking for in Northern California: Elms? Eucalyptus? Maples? I rushed to the body copy at the bottom of the page breathlessly searching for the answer. It never came. Indeed, there was no further reference to trees whatsoever in the advertisement, save a rather obtuse connection to trees in the name of the clothing store—called the Timberland Store.

I phoned the Timberland Store in Sausalito and asked to speak to the manager.

"Hi, my name is Bob Pritikin and I wonder if you could give me some information about your full page newspaper ad with the headline about redwoods."

"I'm sorry I'm not at liberty to give out any information, why do you want to know?"

I explained to the manager, a Ms. Shelly Glasgow, that I was working on a book about advertising. Sensing that I would be laudatory about her marvelous whitespace ad, she became very cooperative.

"The ad did an excellent job," she volunteered, "the store was packed."

"How many people, Ms. Glasgow, would you say came into the store as a direct result of the ad?"

"Twenty," she said.

"Twenty?" I wasn't sure I had heard correctly.

"Twenty," she confirmed, "and oh, we must have gotten at least thirty phone calls!"

Between her glee and my incredulity—I thought it best to terminate the phone conversation as quickly as possible.

As most of Northern California was drowning in Ms. Glasgow's sea of white space—it is perhaps reassuring to know that at least 20 people stayed afloat long enough to swim over to the opening of The Timberland Store. The $15,545 ad cost the Timberland Store $777.25 to attract each of the 20 customers.

The thought occurs to me that she could have attracted the same number of customer prospects with a few two line classified ads.

Next time you spend money on a retail newspaper ad be a cheap skate. Pretend your ad layout has a skate key attached to it and start tightening the key. Keep turning the key until you have squeezed all of the needless space out of your ad. And not just whitespace, squeeze out the needless information, too.

The following examples, beginning overleaf on pages 178 and 179, were fabricated with scissors and glue by master layout technician Tony Eglin, to illustrate once again the marvelous opportunity for saving advertising space costs by shrinking ads without sacrificing the impact of the illustration, the size of the type or the number of words.

Since these before and after comparisons to follow require facing pages I will provide you with the ultimate esoteric white space ad on page 177! This two page indulgence in *Interview* magazine cost the advertiser, whoever it might be, $11,920. Have another drink...

L O U I S E   B O U R G E O I S

O S I R I S   E D I T I O N S

the curtain

This Ad Cost $10,143

Doctors hush up AIDS cases

As a result, specialists say, there may be twice as many victims

Knight News Service

MIAMI – Specialists say their fight against AIDS is being hampered by doctors who fail to report cases. They say the number of victims may actually be twice the official count.

In some instances, doctors withhold information they are preparing for prestigious medical journals, where publication often bolsters reputations. These journals often reject articles with information that's already public.

Researchers contend that scientific progress hinges on research that is painstakingly reviewed by fellow specialists. They object to immediate disclosure of raw figures by public health authorities.

But Dr. Richard Selik, who logs cases of acquired immune deficiency syndrome for the federal Centers for Disease Control in Atlanta, insists that failure to report cases threatens to impede the search for the causes and how it spreads.

Worse, he says, withholding information could jeopardize people who are unknowingly at risk. "It impairs our ability to investigate the possibility that some occupations may entail a risk of AIDS. It might mean delays in taking appropriate precautions – and could possibly result in a higher number of cases."

Selik says the CDC allegations are based on reports from local health officials and on the number of orders for a drug. It's called pentamidine and is available solely from the government. The drug is used to treat an unusual type of pneumonia found in AIDS patients.

To improve reporting, federal officials have sent public health advisers to the three states with the largest AIDS outbreaks: New York, California and Florida.

In San Francisco, health officials said reporting is not a problem. Dr. Selma Dritz, chief epidemiologist with the Department of Public Health, said her department gets "excellent" cooperation from physicians, hospitals, clinics and even from people in the gay community who provide leads her office follows up.

"We have one physician quite reluctant to report, but he does, making it possible for us to get an overall listing of patients," said Dritz, who added that the doctor was reluctant to report cases because he was so busy.

She said doctors are legally obligated to report AIDS cases to the state.

Another reason for lower numbers, Dritz said, "is delay. We have been swamped here."

The disease robs the body of its protection against infections. It primarily afflicts homosexual and bisexual men, Haitians, hemophiliacs, and abusers of intravenous drugs.

CDC adviser Gus Sermos says possibly half of all the AIDS cases have not been reported to health authorities.

In many instances, physicians say they are too busy to fill out the CDC's time-consuming forms. Some may also wish to keep patients' personal information confidential – and others want to keep their research secret.

"Some physicians withhold data if they are doing a special research project and want to report their findings first," Selik says.

"There are people who think that AIDS is stock and they can buy into it," Sermos says. "Nobody owns AIDS. This is a public health situation, and when you're talking about public health, you're talking about public death."

Some researchers contend, however, that the alleged reporting problem arises from the CDC's ineptitude in gathering and handling available data. Tallies of sexually transmitted diseases are equally inaccurate, they say.

They accuse the CDC epidemiologists, whose job is to monitor disease patterns, of releasing confidential scientific data hastily in the center's weekly newsletter – which is intended for up-to-the-minute public health reports.

The CDC newsletter, called the Morbidity and Mortality Weekly Report, is the bible of public health physicians. It carries updates on infectious diseases – and occasionally reports new findings.

National digest

Compiled from Examiner news services

Dividend taxes deal sought

WASHINGTON – Congressional tax writers hoped to complete a compromise plan today to repeal the 10 percent tax withholding on interest and dividends and send it to the House and Senate for approval before the Aug. 1 deadline. Negotiators tentatively agreed on the withholding compromise last night but fell short of final approval when they deadlocked over a rider to extend state and local governments authority to issue tax-exempt mortgage bonds that expires at the end of the year. They also attached an administration-backed Caribbean aid package to the withholding repealer to enhance its chances of presidential approval.

Plane crashes kill 9 in East

NINE PEOPLE DIED in plane crashes in Cleveland and Lost Creek, W.Va., yesterday. Authorities fear the death toll from Cleveland crash may increase to six. They are trying to determine the identities of at least five people killed in the crash of a twin-engine Aero Commander that scattered parts of bodies over 150 yards in a Cleveland industrial park. A Piper Navajo carrying four Texans slammed into a field in West Virginia and burned minutes after takeoff from Clarksburg Benedum Airport, killing all aboard.

Times Beach asks more

WASHINGTON – The government has spent $36.5 million to buy out dioxin-contaminated Times Beach, Mo., but the city's mayor says the sum is too small to compensate residents whose hometown became "a national symbol of something unclean." Mayor Marilyn Leistner told Congress yesterday she appreciated the government's help. But she suggested that it also impose a tax on chemicals to help provide health care for people suffering from exposure to dioxin and other toxic chemicals.

Death voted for U.S. Nazi

CLEVELAND – A jury has recommended the death sentence for Frank Spisak, an avowed Nazi convicted of killing two blacks and a man he thought was Jewish. Following the jury's recommendation yesterday, Spisak told his lawyer he wants to be electrocuted as soon as possible. The same jury last week convicted Spisak in the 1982 murders of three men on the campus of Cleveland State University. During the trial, Spisak testified he was waging a guerrilla war against blacks and Jews and said it made no difference how many of them were slain.

Quintuple-slaying charges

LAKE ARTHUR, La. – First-degree murder charges were filed against an ex-mental patient who had terrorized his family in the past and now is accused of killing his parents, brother and two other relatives. Federal officials along the U.S.-Mexico border were hunting for Michael Owen Perry, 28, in Louisiana and Texas. The bullet-riddled bodies of his parents and his 2-year-old nephew were discovered Tuesday in their southwest Louisiana house and the bodies of a brother and a cousin were found at another residence two doors away, officials said.

Transplant hopeful dies

ELEVEN-YEAR-OLD Michelle Heckard died yesterday while awaiting a donor for lifesaving liver transplant. Michelle of Shenandoah, Pa., died in Philadelphia's Childrens' Hospital of cirrhosis of the liver after lapsing into a coma Monday, a hospital spokesman said. Doctors had been unable to find a donor organ for her. Doctors in Salt Lake City and Minneapolis tried to find livers to save two other critically ill children. Doctors at the University of Minnesota Hospital thought they had found a donor liver yesterday for Adriane Broderick, 2, of Minden, La., but it proved to be unacceptable. Clayton Conger of Rock Springs, Wyo., is being treated the University of Utah Medical Center for alpha 1-anti-trypsin deficiency, a rare disease that strikes fewer than one in 2,000 children. The disease, a hereditary protein deficiency, is destroying the child's liver.

Same Ad-Cut Down Version Saves $1691

Thurs., July 21, 1[illegible] • S.F. EXAMINER A7

Doctors hush up AIDS cases

As a result, specialists say, there may be twice as many victims

Knight News Service

MIAMI – Specialists say their fight against AIDS is being hampered by doctors who fail to report cases. They say the number of victims may actually be twice the official count.

In some instances, doctors withhold information they are preparing for prestigious medical journals, where publication often bolsters reputations. These journals often reject articles with information that's already public.

Researchers contend that scientific progress hinges on research that is painstakingly reviewed by fellow specialists. They object to immediate disclosure of raw figures by public health authorities.

But Dr. Richard Selik, who logs cases of acquired immune deficiency syndrome for the federal Centers for Disease Control in Atlanta, insists that failure to report cases threatens to impede the search for the causes and how it spreads.

Worse, he says, withholding information could jeopardize people who are unknowingly at risk. "It impairs our ability to investigate the possibility that some occupations may entail a risk of AIDS. It might mean delays in taking appropriate precautions – and could possibly result in a higher number of cases."

Selik says the CDC allegations are based on reports from local health officials and on the number of orders for a drug. It's called pentamidine and is available solely from the government. The drug is used to treat an unusual type of pneumonia found in AIDS patients.

To improve reporting, federal officials have sent public health advisers to the three states with the largest AIDS outbreaks: New York, California and Florida.

In San Francisco, health officials said reporting is not a problem. Dr. Selma Dritz, chief epidemiologist with the Department of Public Health, said her department gets "excellent" cooperation from physicians, hospitals, clinics and even from people in the gay community who provide leads her office follows up.

"We have one physician quite reluctant to report, but he does, making it possible for us to get an overall line listing of patients," said Dritz, who added that the doctor was reluctant to report cases because he was so busy.

She said doctors are legally obligated to report AIDS cases to the state.

Another reason for lower numbers, Dritz said, "is delay. We have been swamped here."

The disease robs the body of its protection against infections. It primarily afflicts homosexual and bisexual men, Haitians, hemophiliacs, and abusers of intravenous drugs.

CDC adviser Gus Sermos says possibly half of all the AIDS cases have not been reported to health authorities.

In many instances, physicians say they are too busy to fill out the CDC's time consuming forms. Some may also wish to keep patients' personal information confidential – and others want to keep their research secret.

"Some physicians withhold data if they are doing a special research project and want to report their findings first," Selik says.

"There are people who think that AIDS is stock and they can buy into it," Sermos says. "Nobody owns AIDS. This is a public-health situation, and when you're talking about public health, you're talking about public death."

Some researchers contend, however, that the alleged reporting problem arises from the CDC's ineptitude in gathering and handling available data. Tallies of sexually transmitted diseases are equally inaccurate, they say.

They accuse the CDC epidemiologists, whose job is to monitor disease patterns, of releasing confidential scientific data hastily in the center's weekly newsletter – which is intended for up-to-the minute public health reports.

The CDC newsletter, called the Morbidity and Mortality Weekly Report, is the bible of public health physicians. It carries updates on infectious diseases – and occasionally reports new findings.

National digest

Compiled from Examiner news services

Dividend taxes deal sought

WASHINGTON – Congressional tax writers hoped to complete a compromise plan today to repeal the 10 percent tax withholding on interest and dividends and send it to the House and Senate for approval before the Aug. 1 deadline. Negotiators tentatively agreed on the withholding compromise last night, but fell short of final approval when they deadlocked over a rider to extend state and local governments authority to issue tax-exempt mortgage bonds that expires at the end of the year. They also attached an administration-backed Caribbean aid package to the withholding repealer to enhance its chances of presidential approval.

Plane crashes kill 9 in East

NINE PEOPLE DIED in plane crashes in Cleveland and Lost Creek, W.Va., yesterday. Authorities fear the death toll from Cleveland crash may increase to six. They are trying to determine the identities of at least five people killed in the crash of a twin-engine Aero Commander that scattered parts of bodies over 150 yards in a Cleveland industrial park. A Piper Navajo carrying four Texans slammed into a field in West Virginia and burned minutes after takeoff from Clarksburg Benedum Airport, killing all aboard.

Times Beach asks more

WASHINGTON – The government has spent $36.5 million to buy out dioxin-contaminated Times Beach, Mo., but the city's mayor says the sum is too small to compensate residents whose hometown became "a national symbol of something unclean." Mayor Marilyn Leistner told Congress yesterday she appreciated the government's help. But she suggested that it also impose a tax on chemicals to help provide health care for people suffering from exposure to dioxin and other toxic chemicals.

Death voted for U.S. Nazi

CLEVELAND – A jury has recommended the death sentence for Frank Spisak, an avowed Nazi convicted of killing two blacks and a man he thought was Jewish. Following the jury's recommendation yesterday, Spisak told his lawyer he wants to be electrocuted as soon as possible. The same jury last week convicted Spisak in the 1982 murders of three men on the campus of Cleveland State University. During the trial, Spisak testified he was waging a guerrilla war against blacks and Jews and said it made no difference how many of them were slain.

Quintuple-slaying charges

LAKE ARTHUR, La. – First-degree murder charges were filed against an ex-mental patient who had terrorized his family in the past and now is accused of killing his parents, brother and two other relatives. Federal officials along the U.S.-Mexico border were hunting for Michael Owen Perry, 28, in Louisiana and Texas. The bullet-riddled bodies of his parents and his 2-year-old nephew were discovered Tuesday in their southwest Louisiana house and the bodies of a brother and a cousin were found at another residence two doors away, officials said.

Transplant hopeful dies

ELEVEN-YEAR-OLD Michelle Heckard died yesterday while awaiting a donor for lifesaving liver transplant. Michelle of Shenandoah, Pa., died in Philadelphia's Childrens' Hospital of cirrhosis of the liver after lapsing into a coma Monday, a hospital spokesman said. Doctors had been unable to find a donor organ for her. Doctors in Salt Lake City and Minneapolis tried to find livers to save two other critically ill children. Doctors at the University of Minnesota Hospital thought they had found a donor liver yesterday for Adriane Broderick, 2, of Minden, La., but it proved to be unacceptable. Clayton Conger of Rock Springs, Wyo., is being treated the University of Utah Medical Center for alpha-1-anti-trypsin deficiency, a rare disease that strikes fewer than one in 2,000 children. The disease, a hereditary protein deficiency, is destroying the child's liver.

Florida's Theory on AIDS 'Dumping'

By Randy Shilts

The Florida health department said yesterday that fear among medical personnel of getting AIDS may have caused the curious transfer of an AIDS patient from Gainesville to San Francisco.

Morgan MacDonald, hospitalized for almost three months in Florida for treatment of acquired immune deficiency syndrome, was flown on a Learjet to San Francisco last Tuesday and placed on the

opportunity within the law to avoid providing care," he said.

Pietrodangelo said the state government would take no action because "this was the action of one private hospital and did not in any way represent the policy of the state of Florida. This is an isolated instance."

Silverman said that he had heard of MacDonald's case even before the sick man arrived in San Francisco, because Florida social workers had contacted both the in-

A week later, an ambulance pulled in front of the foundation's office on 10th Street and MacDonald was loaded on a guerney, pushed into the offices and deposited on the foundation's floor with a few plastic bags containing all his belongings.

"We were expecting a car or a cab, because they said he was ambulatory," said Power. "It was obvious from the start that he was real out of it. He couldn't even walk. The man needed hospitalization."

recuperative phase," according to Hunt, who said she participated in the discussions surrounding MacDonald's case. "He walked out of the hospital and he walked onto the plane."

Hunt said the social workers who arranged the flight were on vacation and not available for comment, but that they were "adament" that they had told the truth to the San Francisco personnel.

"I'm in a [illegible]andary over all the controv[illegible]," she [illegible]. "His prob-

Pumping had begun Friday evening after the Army Corps of Engineers granted a permit. Its issuance was opposed by sports fishermen and environmentalists on grounds that white bass could get past a newly built fish screen four miles above Tulare Lake and wreck the salmon and striped bass fisheries of the San Joaquin-Sacramento river network.

The poisoning operation drew new criticism from the Kings County fishermen and also raised concerns about the possible threat to delta drinking water supplies.

"Fishing people are very much outraged," said [illegible] J. Meirelles of Hanford, the only member of the

assistant deputy health chief with the California Occupational Safety and Health Administration, said, "I don't think it's safe to give the fish away. They should be destroyed."

Greenberg said rotenone has been known to cause cancer in laboratory experiments with rats, although there has been no evidence of harmful effects on humans.

"They're putting poison into water that could go to the delta, which is a drinking water source for 15 million people," he said, "and no pumping should be allowed until not a trace of rotenone can be detected."

White said pumping would [illegible]

Grodins

LOWEST PRICE
OF THE SEASON
INCLUDING MANY
SUITS NEVER
BEFORE REDUCED

SAVE $116. . . DOMINIC D'BRUZZI

MEN'S PURE WOOL VESTED SUITS

$209

Our regular $325 pure wool vested D'Bruzzi suit. Superb imported woolens in stripes, plaids and solid shades. Carefully tailored to assure you a fine fit and long wear. The quality and workmanship are outstanding. A fantastic value at this very special price! We invite you to shop and compare this exceptional value! Compare the fabrics. Compare the workmanship. Compare the price. We think this suit is the best for the money in the state! And it's a Grodins exclusive! Pant cuffs are free, charge for other alterations on sale clothing.

Stockton/Market, Embarcadero, Stonestown, Serramonte, Northgate, Larkspur Landing, Santa Rosa Plaza

This Ad Cost $10,143

Thurs., Aug. 11, 19' S.F. EXAMINER A7

Air Force denies missile story

NEW YORK (AP) — The Air Force has called "completely false" a report that a Titan missile, armed with a nuclear warhead, went into its launch sequence during a 1980 test and was nearly fired by mistake.

In a report to be published Sunday in Parade magazine, columnist Jack Anderson bases the report on statements by launch officer David Mosley, a first lieutenant who was assigned to McConnell Air Force Base near Wichita.

Mosley told the columnist that a Titan missile went into its launch sequence during a test on Nov. 19, 1980, but Mosley said his partner, Capt. Henry Winsett, "pulled the plug" to prevent the missile from taking off.

Yesterday, the Air Force said the story was untrue.

"Any reports or allegations of an 'inadvertent launch of a Titan II' potential during this time at this complex are completely false," said Air Force spokeswoman Capt. Virginia Pribyla.

The missile's nuclear warhead and guidance devices had been removed before the test, she said, and so had the explosive charges that ignite the missile fuel.

Mosley told Anderson that during the test he and Winsett turned the proper keys, but "strange things" began happening.

"We had a green light on the butterfly valve lock control that was not supposed to have a light at all," Mosley said.

"Instead of giving us the lights that said the test had begun, it said, 'Launch OK' and 'Launch Systems Go,' which means you're actually in the launch sequence," Mosley said. He said Winsett then aborted the sequence.

The Air Force statement said the test is intended to run through the launch procedure, "monitoring each light as it indicates a correct launch sequence ending with 'liftoff' lighted."

The test cited by Anderson, the Air Force said, "had no special problems or circumstances associated with it."

Confessed mass-murderer fit for trial

MONTAGUE, Texas (AP) — A drifter who claims to have killed 100 women in 16 states was ruled mentally competent yesterday to stand trial on charges he killed an 80-year-old woman.

Henry Lee Lucas nodded when asked by state District Judge Frank Douthitt if he agreed with the mental competency ruling.

He has said he killed women in Texas, New Mexico, Arizona, Utah, California, Oregon, South Dakota, Minnesota, Illinois, Michigan, West Virginia, Florida, Louisiana, New Jersey, Oklahoma and Missouri.

Douthitt said his ruling was based on reports from three psychiatrists that the 46-year-old former mental patient was competent to aid in his defense.

Douthitt set trial for Sept. 13 in the slaying of Kate Rich of nearby Ringgold. Pretrial motions will be heard Sept. 7.

One motion pending is by defense lawyer Don Maxfield calling for the trial to be moved because of strong sentiment in Montague County against Lucas, who has been charged with five Texas killings.

Lucas is being held on $1 million bond in Montague County. He began talking about the slayings of other women after he was charged in Rich's slaying.

He also has been charged in the death of his 15-year-old traveling companion, Frieda Powell, a runaway from Jacksonville, Fla., whose remains were found in Denton County.

Lucas subsequently was charged in the slayings of an unidentified woman whose headless body was found near Plainview in February 1982 and the March 1981 strangulation of Beverly Joyce Luttrell, a 48-year-old Odessa woman.

National digest

Compiled from Examiner news services

Drug angle in campus killing

BOULDER, Colo. — The slain boyfriend of Robert Redford's daughter had been selling cocaine and "may have gotten into something over his head," according to one of his roommates. Thayne Smika said late yesterday that 22-year-old Sidney L. Wells "was dealing coke," the Rocky Mountain News reported today. Smika, 24, also said that he didn't shoot Wells, his roommate in a posh condominium near the University of Colorado. Wells, the longtime boyfriend of Shauna Redford, was found shot to death Aug. 1. An autopsy found that Wells died from a single shotgun blast to the back of his head. Smika refused to comment when asked if he used or sold cocaine with Wells, a senior majoring in broadcast journalism at the University of Colorado.

$115,000 angel for quints

BERNARDS TOWNSHIP, N.J. — The father of the Kienast quintuplets says the family is "going to smile a lot" after being given more than $115,000 to keep their house. William Kienast said yesterday "one source" gave his family the money he used to pay off three mortgages totaling more than $97,000 and another $17,900 in property taxes. By paying off the debts, the Kienasts redeemed the eight-bedroom house on four acres in this Somerset County community one day before an auction sale would have become final. The family began to suffer financial problems in the early 1970s when Kienast's business, extruding plastic sheets to manufacture eyeglass frames, faltered.

CAB probes computers

WASHINGTON — The Civil Aeronautics Board is investigating whether three competing airline computer reservation systems are designed to give any one airline a boost over its competitors. The agency began investigating the systems yesterday. They are now used by about 80 percent of all travel agents. The reservations process is handled through three major systems run by three big airlines: United's Apollo system, American's Saber system and TWA's Pars system. The fairness question arises because 80 percent of the computerized agents use systems sold or leased by either American Airlines or United Airlines. Other airlines have alleged that American and United use the computer systems to manipulate schedule and fare information.

Crane tells contrition

DANVILLE, Ill. — In his first home appearance since a July 20 censure by the U.S. House, Rep. Daniel B. Crane said that if constituents can't forgive him for having sex with a 17-year-old page, then they "have a prerogative, come March, to vote me out." Crane drew repeated ovations from sparse, home-district crowds yesterday as he addressed voters. "I know I did wrong," the 47-year-old Republican told the only person who asked about the page scandal. "I've confessed and asked forgiveness of my God, my wife and my children," he said with his wife, Judy, at his side. Crane told members of a crowd in Danville that they should judge him on his House record and that his Capitol Hill colleagues have urged him to seek a fourth term.

AIDS fear blocks aid for tot

ORLANDO, Fla. A father fearful of AIDS refuses to let his infant son have a transfusion of anyone's blood but his, and blood bank officials say they won't allow a "direct transfusion." Richard Studer offered his own blood to his 11-month-old son, Robert, yesterday because he fears the mysterious disease AIDS, acquired immune deficiency syndrome, is spread by blood transfusions. But Central Florida Blood Bank officials said "direct transfusions" such as the kind Studer wants to give are against policies established nationally by blood banks. Studer's boy was hospitalized at the Orlando Regional Medical Center for an intestinal disorder that left him malnourished and in need of periodic transfusions.

Same Ad-Cut Down Version Saves $1691

Thurs., Aug. 11, 19.. S.F. EXAMINER A7

Air Force denies missile story

NEW YORK (AP) — The Air Force has called "completely false" a report that a Titan missile, armed with a nuclear warhead, went into its launch sequence during a 1980 test and was nearly fired by mistake.

In a report to be published Sunday in Parade magazine, columnist Jack Anderson bases the report on statements by launch officer David Mosley, a first lieutenant who was assigned to McConnell Air Force Base near Wichita.

Mosley told the columnist that a Titan missile went into its launch sequence during a test on Nov. 19, 1980, but Mosley said his partner, Capt. Henry Winsett "pulled the plug" to prevent the missile from taking off.

Yesterday, the Air Force said the story was untrue.

"Any reports or allegations of an 'inadvertent launch of a Titan II' potential during this time at this complex are completely false," said Air Force spokeswoman Capt. Virginia Pribyla.

The missile's nuclear warhead and guidance devices had been removed before the test, she said, and so had the explosive charges that ignite the missile fuel.

Mosley told Anderson that during the test he and Winsett turned the proper keys, but "strange things" began happening.

"We had a green light on the butterfly valve lock control that was not supposed to have a light at all," Mosley said.

"Instead of giving us the lights that said the test had begun, it said, 'Launch OK' and 'Launch Systems Go,' which means you're actually in the launch sequence," Mosley said. He said Winsett then aborted the sequence.

The Air Force statement said the test is intended to run through the launch procedure, "monitoring each light as it indicates a correct launch sequence ending with 'liftoff' lighted."

The test cited by Anderson, the Air Force said, "had no special problems or circumstances associated with it."

Confessed mass-murderer fit for trial

MONTAGUE, Texas (AP) — A drifter who claims to have killed 100 women in 16 states was ruled mentally competent yesterday to stand trial on charges he killed an 80-year-old woman.

Henry Lee Lucas nodded when asked by state District Judge Frank Douthitt if he agreed with the mental competency ruling.

He has said he killed women in Texas, New Mexico, Arizona, Utah, California, Oregon, South Dakota, Minnesota, Illinois, Michigan, West Virginia, Florida, Louisiana, New Jersey, Oklahoma and Missouri.

Douthitt said his ruling was based on reports from three psychiatrists that the 46-year-old former mental patient was competent to aid in his defense.

Douthitt set trial for Sept. 13 in the slaying of Kate Rich of nearby Ringgold. Pretrial motions will be heard Sept. 7.

One motion pending is by defense lawyer Don Maxfield calling for the trial to be moved because of strong sentiment in Montague County against Lucas, who has been charged with five Texas killings.

Lucas is [illegible] million bond in Montague County. He began talking about the slayings of other women after he was charged in Rich's slaying.

He also has been charged in the death of his 15-year-old traveling companion, Frieda Powell, a runaway from Jacksonville, Fla., whose remains were found in Denton County.

Lucas subsequently was charged in the slayings of an unidentified woman whose headless body was found near Plainview in February 1982 and the March 1981 strangulation of Beverly Joyce Luttrell, a 46-year-old Odessa woman.

National digest

Compiled from Examiner news services

Drug angle in campus killing

BOULDER, Colo. — The slain boyfriend of Robert Redford's daughter had been selling cocaine and "may have gotten into something over his head," according to one of his roommates. Thayne Smika said late yesterday that 22-year-old Sidney J. Wells "was dealing coke," the Rocky Mountain News reported today. Smika, 24, also said that he didn't shoot Wells, his roommate in a posh condominium near the University of Colorado. Wells, the longtime boyfriend of Shauna Redford, was found shot to death Aug. 1. An autopsy found that Wells died from a single shotgun blast to the back of his head. Smika refused to comment when asked if he used or sold cocaine with Wells, a senior majoring in broadcast journalism at the University of Colorado.

$115,000 angel for quints

BERNARDS TOWNSHIP, N.J. — The father of the Kienast quintuplets says the family is "going to smile a lot" after being given more than $115,000 to keep their house. William Kienast said yesterday "one source" gave his family the money he used to pay off three mortgages totaling more than $97,000 and another $17,900 in property taxes. By paying off the debts, the Kienasts redeemed the eight-bedroom house on four acres in this Somerset County community one day before an auction sale would have become final. The family began to suffer financial problems in the early 1970s when Kienast's business, extruding plastic sheets to manufacture eyeglass frames, faltered.

CAB probes computers

WASHINGTON — The Civil Aeronautics Board is investigating whether three competing airline computer reservation [illegible] to give any one airline a boost over its competitors. The agency began investigating the systems yesterday. They are now used by about 8[illegible] percent of all travel agents. The reservations process is handled through three major systems run by three big airlines: United's Apollo system, American's Saber system and TWA's Pars system. The fairness question arises because 80 percent of the computerized agents use systems sold or leased by either American Airlines or United Airlines. Other airlines have alleged that American and United use the computer systems to manipulate schedule and fare information.

Crane tells contrition

DANVILLE, Ill. — In his first home appearance since a July 20 censure by the U.S. House, Rep. Daniel B. Crane said that if constituents can't forgive him for having sex with a 17-year-old page, then they "have a prerogative, come March, to vote me out." Crane drew repeated ovations from sparse, home-district crowds yesterday as he addressed voters. "I know I did wrong," the 47-year-old Republican told the only person who asked about the page scandal. "I've confessed and asked forgiveness of my God, my wife and my children," he said with his wife, Judy, at his side. Crane told members of a crowd in Danville that they should judge him on his House record and that his Capitol Hill colleagues have urged him to seek a fourth term.

AIDS fear blocks aid for tot

ORLANDO, Fla. A father fearful of AIDS refuses to let his infant son have a transfusion of anyone's blood but his, and blood bank officials say they won't allow a "direct transfusion." Richard Studer offered his own blood to his 11-month-old son Robert yesterday because he fears the mysterious disease AIDS, acquired immune deficiency syndrome, is spread by blood transfusions. But Central Florida Blood Bank officials said "direct transfusions" such as the kind Studer wants to give are against policies established nationally by blood banks. Studer's boy was hospitalized at the Orlando Regional Medical Center for an intestinal disorder that left him malnourished and in need of periodic transfusions.

Administration Proposes Tightening of Medicaid

Washington

The Reagan administration is seeking changes in the Medicaid program that would give states new power to restrict eligibility and to reduce benefits for thousands of children and elderly people with high medical expenses.

The proposed changes would apply to people with low incomes who would be impoverished if they had to pay all their medical expenses.

Federal officials said that 3.7 million of the 21.9 million Medicaid recipients are in this category, which includes 795,000 de-

yer at Legal Services for the Elderly in New York City, said the rules could "deny Medicaid coverage to many people below or slightly above the poverty level."

The federal poverty level for one person in 1982 was $4901 in annual income, and a person with an average monthly income of less than $408 was classified as poor.

James D. Weill, legal director of the Children's Defense Fund, said that in issuing the rule proposals, the administration was "ignoring the will of Congress."

"These changes," he added, "would force many children and their families either to forgo medical care or to spend more of their own money on medical care, leaving less of their meager income for food, clothing and shelter."

In the fiscal year 1982, federal and state agencies spent a total of $29.9 billion on Medicaid, including $8.3 billion for the medically needy, according to data collected by the federal government. Total program costs grew at an average rate of more than 16 percent a year from 1974 through 1980.

The Reagan administration said it did not have a precise estimate of the savings that might result from the new rules. However, it said the total savings would be less than $500 million a year. One change, related to the reimbursement of nursing homes, is expected to save $18 million a year.

The new rules would not affect Medicare, the health insurance program for the elderly. Medicaid is intended for people with little or no income, and Medicare is for almost everyone age 65 or older, regardless of income.

The public has until November 1 to comment on the proposed rules. Congress could attempt to block them by passing legislation. In addition, states could block the rules by not using their power to restrict eligibility. But in the last two years states have been searching for ways to control Medicaid costs, the largest single item in many state budgets.

Under another of the new rules, states could disregard outstanding bills for services rendered to a person more than three months before he or she applied for Medicaid. Lawyers for Medicaid recipients said the three-month limit would penalize poor people for a hospital's slowness in sending bills. Many people, the lawyers said, turn to Medicaid for assistance when they find themselves unable to pay old medical bills.

New York Times

This Ad Cost $10,143

San Francisco Chronicle 7
Thurs., July 28, 19

Deukmejian Action

Toxic Waste Fund Cuts Denounced

By Bill Soiffer

A coalition of 16 environmental, labor and public interest groups charged yesterday that Governor Deukmejian cut more than a $1.7 million in toxic substances control programs that are supported by fees from waste disposal firms.

Michael Belliveau, director of the Hazardous Waste Program of Citizens for a Better Environment, said the toxic control programs would have been financed not by state taxes but through the Hazardous Waste Control Account, a fund that collects fees on hazardous waste disposal.

"These budget actions seem to directly contradict the governor's earlier statements that hazardous wastes are the No 1 environmental problem facing our state today and that he is committed to controlling the problem," said Belliveau. "The only rationale is that big industry didn't want their fees going for new programs."

Belliveau said that it was unclear to him where the fees in the Hazardous Waste Control Account will be redirected.

In a letter to the governor, Belliveau warned that toxic chemical pollution will continue to pose serious public health and environmental threats for years to come unless these cuts are reconsidered.

Joel Moscowitz, the newly appointed head of the state Toxic Substances Control Program, agreed the programs would have been financed from fees imposed on hazardous waste disposal. But he said he was unable to explain or comment on the cuts in the program because he was appointed only five weeks ago.

Moscowitz said the Hazardous Waste Control Account collected $900,000 less than the $5.5 million that was anticipated last year. But the Legislature recently increased hazardous waste disposal fees from $4 per ton to a two-tiered schedule of $18 per ton for highly toxic hazardous waste and $6.40 per ton for other hazardous waste.

Moscowitz noted that the increased fees are projected to bring in $9.2 million and were supposed to finance the cut programs as well as 21 staff positions to issue toxic waste permits and inspect toxic waste sites.

Any surplus in the Hazardous Waste Control Account, which is used largely to finance emergency cleanups of toxic substances, will be reviewed in setting the fee schedule next year, Moscowitz said.

Evan Nossoff of the State Water Resources Control Board said he didn't believe the $1 million cut in funds to investigate leaking chemical storage tanks was a lost cause yet because of a bill under debate in the Legislature that would restore the money.

GOVERNOR'S CUTS

- $1 million to investigate leaking chemical storage tanks that contaminate water supplies
- $300,000 to expand monitoring of drinking water supplies for toxic chemicals
- $200,000 to study chemical contamination of water caused by the use of plastic pipes
- $264,000 for six staff positions to develop toxic substances control policies

Governor OKs Easing Of Pesticide Controls

Sacramento

Governor Deukmejian signed legislation to weaken the regulation of pesticide use but vetoed a bill to broaden the Legislature's powers over administrative regulations, the governor's office reported yesterday.

Three bills signed by Deukmejian will modify requirements for obtaining permits to use pesticides and require the Department of Food and Agriculture to give reasons for refusing to register pesticides that are registered with the federal government.

In vetoing the regulations bill, Deukmejian said it could violate the constitutional principle of separation of powers by restricting his administration's authority to review state rules and regulations.

The bill by Assemblyman Gary Condit, D-Ceres, would have required the state Office of Administrative Law — run by a Deukmejian appointee — to consider the Legislature's opinions when approving or rejecting the administration's emergency regulations.

Deukmejian signed 23 other bills, including one to give libraries and store owners authority to recover civil damages up to $500 from adults and emancipated minors convicted of stealing property.

Under current law, parents are liable for civil damages up to $500 if their children are convicted of shoplifting or stealing library books.

The three pesticide bills signed by the governor were:

- A measure by Assemblyman Wally Herger, R-Rio Oso, to limit requirements for pesticide permits to cases when pesticides are registered as restricted materials. Use of non-restricted pesticides will no longer require a permit unless the county agricultural commissioner determines that an undue hazard will exist when the material is used.
- A bill also by Herger requiring the department director to give reasons when refusing to register pesticides or other poisons that already are registered by the U.S. Environmental Protection Agency.
- A measure by Assemblyman Eric Seastrand, R-Salinas, requiring those who use pesticides on their own property or the property of neighbors to have a license, but waiving the regular business license fee of $50.

United Press

Lawyers' Fees Big Chunk of Asbestos Suits

Washington

Lawyers' fees and other legal costs consume 63 percent of all money paid out by defendants in asbestos law suits, leaving 37 percent to compensate injured plaintiffs, according to a study released yesterday.

In their study of 24,000 law suits, researchers at Rand Corp found that the victims keep an average of $35,000 out of the average award of $60,000. The rest goes to the victim's lawyers.

But defendants spend about $35,000 on attorneys to fight each suit, bringing the defendant's total cost on the average case to $95,000.

Of the $1 billion in costs paid out to date in these suits, the report said, two-thirds was paid by insurers and one-third by defendants.

Asbestos is used in insulation and cement products, brake linings and roofing and flooring products. Asbestos fibers, when inhaled, can lead to lung and chest cancer or asbestosis.

United Press

Same Ad-Cut Down Version Saves $2029

San Francisco Chronicle 7 · Thurs., July 28, 1983

Deukmejian Action

Toxic Waste Fund Cuts Denounced

By Bill Soiffer

A coalition of 16 environmental, labor and public interest groups charged yesterday that Governor Deukmejian cut more than a $1.7 million in toxic substances control programs that are supported by fees from waste disposal firms.

Michael Belliveau, director of the Hazardous Waste Program of Citizens for a Better Environment, said the toxic control programs would have been financed not by state taxes but through the Hazardous Waste Control Account, a fund that collects fees on hazardous waste disposal.

"These budget actions seem to directly contradict the governor's earlier statements that hazardous wastes are the No. 1 environmental problem facing our state today and that he is committed to controlling the problem," said Belliveau. "The only rationale is that big industry didn't want their fees going for new programs."

Belliveau said that it was unclear to him where the fees in the Hazardous Waste Control Account will be redirected.

In a letter to the governor, Belliveau warned that toxic chemical pollution will continue to pose serious public health and environmental threats for years to come unless these cuts are reconsidered.

Joel Moscowitz, the newly appointed head of the state Toxic Substances Control Program, agreed the programs would have been financed from fees imposed on hazardous waste disposal. But he said he was unable to explain or comment on the cuts in the program because he was appointed only five weeks ago.

Moscowitz said the Hazardous Waste Control Account collected $900,000 less than the $5.5 million that was anticipated last year. But the Legislature recently increased hazardous waste disposal fees from $4 per ton to a two-tiered schedule of $18 per ton for highly toxic hazardous waste and $6.40 per ton for other hazardous waste.

Moscowitz noted that the increased fees are projected to bring in $9.2 million and were supposed to finance the cut programs as well as 21 staff positions to issue toxic waste permits and inspect toxic waste sites.

Any surplus in the Hazardous Waste Control Account, which is used largely to finance emergency cleanups of toxic substances, will be reviewed in setting the fee schedule next year, Moscowitz said.

Evan Nossoff of the State Water Resources Control Board said he didn't believe the $1 million cut in funds to investigate leaking chemical storage tanks was a lost cause yet because of a bill under debate in the Legislature that would restore the money.

GOVERNOR'S CUTS

- **$1 million to investigate leaking chemical storage tanks that contaminate water supplies**
- **$300,000 to expand monitoring of drinking water supplies for toxic chemicals**
- **$200,000 to study chemical contamination of water caused by the use of plastic pipes**
- **$266,000 for six staff positions to develop toxic substances control policies**

General Lee Ki Baek, chairman of the South Korean Joint Chiefs of Staff, was reported injured.

In all, 16 South Koreans were reported killed, along with at least three Burmese journalists whose identities were not disclosed.

Information was sketchy from Burma, which follows a rigid policy of self-isolation. However, South Korean reporters on the trip said Chun had asked through an aide that the Burmese government conduct an investigation and then "arrest the culprits and severely punish them while exposing the plot instigated by North Korea."

Burma's president, San Yu, issued a statement calling the bombing a "premeditated and dastardly act" by terrorists seeking to disrupt

Governor OKs Easing Of Pesticide Controls

Sacramento

Governor Deukmejian signed legislation to weaken the regulation of pesticide use but vetoed a bill to broaden the Legislature's powers over administrative regulations, the governor's office reported yesterday.

Three bills signed by Deukmejian will modify requirements for obtaining permits to use pesticides and require the Department of Food and Agriculture to give reasons for refusing to register pesticides that are registered with the federal government.

In vetoing the regulations bill, Deukmejian said it could violate the constitutional principle of separation of powers by restricting his administration's authority to review state rules and regulations.

The bill by Assemblyman Gary Condit, D-Ceres, would have required the state Office of Administrative Law — run by a Deukmejian appointee — to consider the Legislature's opinions when approving or rejecting the administration's emergency regulations.

Deukmejian signed 23 other bills, including one to give libraries and store owners authority to recover civil damages up to $500 from adults and emancipated minors convicted of stealing property.

Under current law, parents are liable for civil damages up to $500 if their children are convicted of shoplifting or stealing library books.

The three pesticide bills signed by the governor were:

- A measure by Assemblyman Wally Herger, R-Rio Oso, to limit requirements for pesticide permits to cases when pesticides are registered as restricted materials. Use of non-restricted pesticides will no longer require a permit unless the county agricultural commissioner determines that an undue hazard will exist when the material is used.
- A bill also by Herger requiring the department director to give reasons when refusing to register pesticides or other poisons that already are registered by the U.S. Environmental Protection Agency.
- A measure by Assemblyman Eric Seastrand, R-Salinas, requiring those who use pesticides on their own property or the property of neighbors to have a license, but waiving the regular business license fee of $50.

United Press

Lawyers' Fees Big Chunk of Asbestos Suits

Washington

Lawyers' fees and other legal costs consume 63 percent of all money paid out by defendants in asbestos lawsuits, leaving 37 percent to compensate injured plaintiffs, according to a study released yesterday.

In their study of 24,000 lawsuits, researchers at Rand Corp. found that the victims keep an average of $35,000 out of the average award of $60,000. The rest goes to the victim's lawyers.

But defendants spend about $35,000 on attorneys to fight each suit, bringing the defendant's total cost on the average case to $95,000.

Of the $1 billion in costs paid out to date in these suits, the report said, two-thirds was paid by insurers and one-third by defendants.

Asbestos is used in insulation and cement products, brake linings and roofing and flooring products. Asbestos fibers, when inhaled, can lead to lung and chest cancer or asbestosis.

United Press

WATT RESIGNS POST AS INTERIOR SECRETARY

From Page 1

policy that he promised in his 1981 confirmation hearings. "The restoration of our national parks, refuges and public lands is well under way," he said. "Our actions to reduce the nation's dependency on foreign sources of energy and strategic minerals are working."

He added, "It is time for a new phase of management — one to consolidate the gains we have made. It is my view that my usefulness to you in this administration has come to an end."

Meese, who spoke with Watt [...] little hope that his policies governing national parks, wilderness areas, wildlife refuges, strip mining and other public lands programs will be changed.

"The question now to be answered is whether indeed all of the outrageous policies that have been attributed to Secretary Watt are the policies of Ronald Reagan," said Denny Schaffer, president of the Sierra Club, whose membership has more than doubled since 1981 as part of a grass-roots backlash against Watt's policies.

Rafe Pomerance, head of [...] servation and the Interior Department. Soon after his arrival, the conservative Wyoming native directed what he called "massive changes" in public lands policy.

Without altering the major laws governing more than 700 million acres of federal land, Watt used his discretion as secretary to change the way those lands are managed. He supervised extensive revisions in policies governing strip mining, oil and gas drilling, coal development, national parks, endangered species, wilderness areas, wildlife refuges, more than 300 million [...] mining lands and many other areas of the 750 million-acre public domain.

In the last few months, Congress reined in many of his programs. But in his first two years in office, Watt brought about a significant transfer of government-owned resources to private control. Industry executives generally praised the shift, but conservationists and an increasing number of members of Congress called it a "giveaway," because with energy markets glutted, private companies were able to lease federal minerals at low prices.

This Ad Cost $10,143

Thurs., August 18, 19' • • • • San Francisco Chronicle 7

5 Killed Near Gilroy

Trucker Held in Fatal Crash

By Allyn Stone

A truck driver was arrested for investigation of felony drunken driving and vehicular manslaughter after a head-on collision that killed five people in a van on state highway 152 east of Gilroy yesterday.

Bill Cook, 31, was heading west in a 25-foot rented truck full of fruit when he tried to pass a car on a two-lane stretch of the Pacheco Highway about 5:20 a.m., police said.

Ron Chaffee of the California Highway Patrol said Cook "apparently didn't see" a customized Dodge van approaching.

Two occupants of the van, Antonio Duque, 62, and his wife, Socorro, 51, both of San Jose, were killed instantly in the collision. Two of their granddaughters, Frances Duque, a teenager, and Michelle Duque, 5, were also killed outright.

A third granddaughter, Maria Duque, 7, was critically injured in the wreck. She was taken to Santa Teresa Hospital in San Jose, where she died a short time later.

Chaffee said the impact crushed the cab of the truck and "completely demolished" the van.

The truck rammed a van and sideswiped a car east of Gilroy

Chaffee said the truck also sideswiped the car Cook had been trying to pass, but no one in that car was hurt.

Sheila Ann Freitas, a 26-year-old San Diego woman who was just behind the van, swerved off the road to avoid the crash. Her vehicle overturned but she was uninjured, a CHP spokesman said.

Cook, of Clovis in Fresno County, was injured only slightly. He was arrested at the scene, handcuffed and taken to Santa Clara County Jail for booking.

Highway 152, a major link between U.S. 101 and Interstate 5, was closed until about 3 p.m. to allow accident investigators and cleanup crews to complete their work.

The section of the narrow, twisting highway where the collision occurred has not been recognized as a safety improvement project by the state, even though it has been the scene of 115 fatal traffic accidents since 1970, authorities said.

The state Department of Transportation is about to start preliminary studies for widening an eight-mile stretch of the road from Bell Station to the intersection of Highways 152 and 156.

Vatican Denies Giving OK to Papal Stand-in

Vatican City

The Vatican categorically denied yesterday that it gave permission to an English policeman who looks like Pope John Paul II to impersonate the pontiff for charity.

Bill Bird, a Roman Catholic and member of the Liverpool police force, said that he sent the Vatican photographs of himself and asked permission to dress in papal robes and play the role of the pope to raise money for good causes.

To his amazement, Bird, said, he got the pope's blessing in a Vatican reply to his letter.

"The Holy Father wishes you to know that he appreciates the sentiments. He invokes God's blessing on you," said a letter signed by a monsignor.

The Vatican was amazed by Bird's claim that this was the green light.

"I deny in the most absolute way that authorization of which Mr. Bill Bird speaks has ever been given," Vatican official Don Pierfranco Pastore told reporters.

United Press

Smoking Law Backers Organize S.F. Group

By Evelyn Hsu

A group that includes physicians and environmentalists announced yesterday the formation of a committee to keep San Francisco's strict anti-smoking law on the books.

The law "is to protect the health of people who live and work in San Francisco," said Dr. Ray Weisberg, head of San Franciscans for Local Control, at a press conference on the steps of City Hall.

"Our concern is the public welfare of San Francisco and the integrity of its legislative processes. The tobacco companies' only concern is to sell more cigarets," he said.

The ordinance, which strictly limits smoking in the workplace, is a referendum item on the November ballot. The law says that if non-smokers are not satisfied with an employer's efforts to accommodate smokers and non-smokers, the employer must ban smoking in an office. Employers who fail to comply with the ordinance can be fined up to $500 a day.

The measure, written by Supervisor Wendy Nelder, was signed into law June 4 by Mayor Dianne Feinstein.

Critics who saw the ordinance as divisive, discriminatory and an example of government intrusion organized a drive to put the measure before the voters.

Supporters say the measure falls within the government's responsibility to pass laws protecting health and welfare. "It's the same as sanitation laws," said Weisberg.

The group hopes to raise about $100,000 for its campaign, he said.

The law would not be discriminatory or divisive, said Weisberg, a member of the national board of the American Cancer Society. "It's been done in many places," he said. "Nearly 65 percent of the population are non-smokers. What about discrimination against them in being exposed to harmful health effects."

Others were quick to point out the role of big tobacco companies in the fight to overturn the law.

"If the cigaret companies back on the East Coast hadn't decided to get this repealed, we wouldn't be standing here," said Stanton Glantz, an associate professor of medicine at the University of California's San Francisco Medical Center.

Same Ad-Cut Down Version Saves $2367

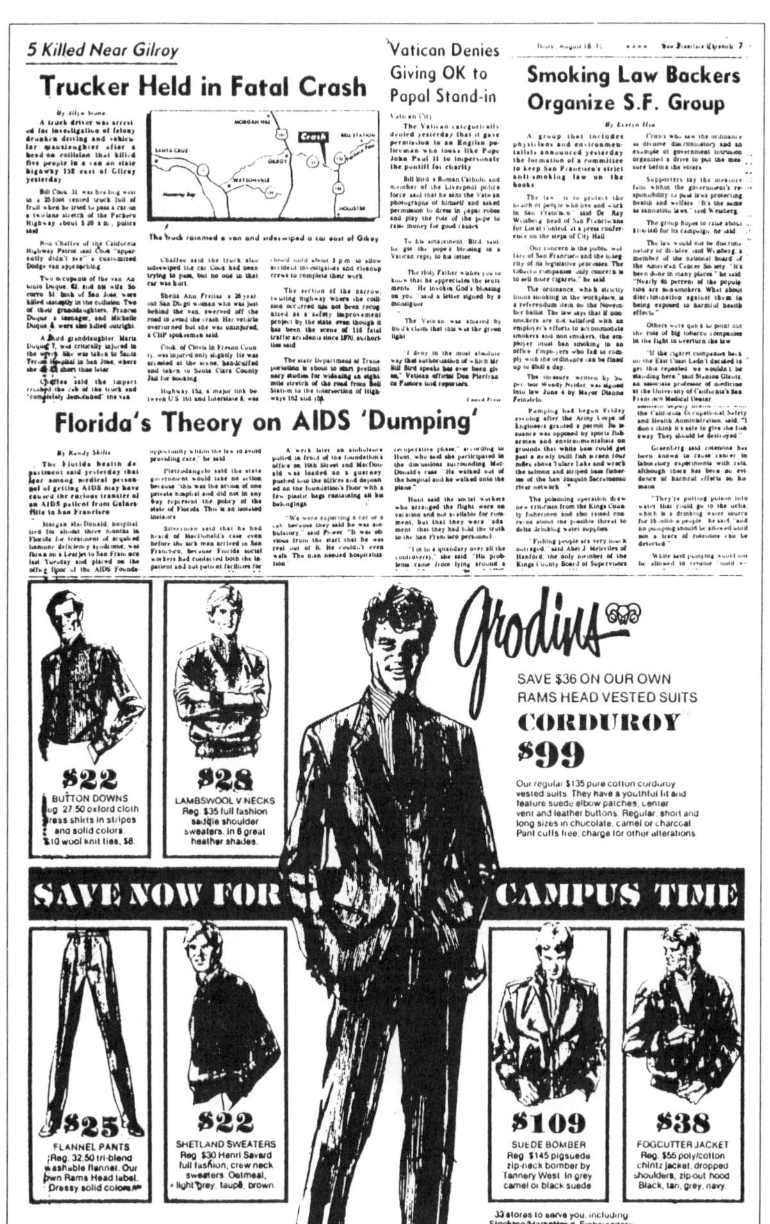

Thurs., August 18, 1[illegible] ★★★★ San Francisco Chronicle 7

5 Killed Near Gilroy

Trucker Held in Fatal Crash

By Allyn Stone

A truck driver was arrested for investigation of felony drunken driving and vehicular manslaughter after a head-on collision that killed five people in a van on state highway 152 east of Gilroy yesterday.

Bill Cook, 31, was heading west in a 25-foot rented truck full of fruit when he tried to pass a car on a two-lane stretch of the Pacheco Highway about 5:20 a.m., police said.

Ron Chaffee of the California Highway Patrol said Cook "apparently didn't see" a customized Dodge van approaching.

Two occupants of the van, Antonio Duque, 62, and his wife, Socorro, 51, both of San Jose, were killed instantly in the collision. Two of their granddaughters, Frances Duque, a teenager, and Michelle Duque, 6, were also killed outright.

A third granddaughter, Maria Duque, 7, was critically injured in the wreck. She was taken to Santa Teresa Hospital in San Jose, where she died a short time later.

Chaffee said the impact crushed the cab of the truck and "completely demolished" the van.

The truck rammed a van and sideswiped a car east of Gilroy

Chaffee said the truck also sideswiped the car Cook had been trying to pass, but no one in that car was hurt.

Sheila Ann Freitas, a 26-year-old San Diego woman who was just behind the van, swerved off the road to avoid the crash. Her vehicle overturned but she was uninjured, a CHP spokesman said.

Cook, of Clovis in Fresno County, was injured only slightly. He was arrested at the scene, handcuffed and taken to Santa Clara County Jail for booking.

Highway 152, a major link between U.S. 101 and Interstate 5, was closed until about 3 p.m. to allow accident investigators and cleanup crews to complete their work.

The section of the narrow, twisting highway where the collision occurred has not been recognized as a safety improvement project by the state, even though it has been the scene of 116 fatal traffic accidents since 1970, authorities said.

The state Department of Transportation is about to start preliminary studies for widening an eight-mile stretch of the road from Bell Station to the intersection of Highways 152 and 156.

Vatican Denies Giving OK to Papal Stand-in

Vatican City

The Vatican categorically denied yesterday that it gave permission to an English policeman who looks like Pope John Paul II to impersonate the pontiff for charity.

Bill Bird, a Roman Catholic and member of the Liverpool police force, said that he sent the Vatican photographs of himself and asked permission to dress in papal robes and play the role of the pope to raise money for good causes.

To his amazement, Bird said, he got the pope's blessing in a Vatican reply to his letter.

"The Holy Father wishes you to know that he appreciates the sentiments. He invokes God's blessing on you," said a letter signed by a monsignor.

The Vatican was amazed by Bird's claim that this was the green light.

"I deny in the most absolute way that authorization of which Mr. Bill Bird speaks has ever been given," Vatican official Don Pierfranco Pastore told reporters.

United Press

Smoking Law Backers Organize S.F. Group

By Evelyn Hsu

A group that includes physicians and environmentalists announced yesterday the formation of a committee to keep San Francisco's strict anti-smoking law on the books.

"The law ... is to protect the health of people who live and work in San Francisco," said Dr. Ray Weisberg, head of San Franciscans for Local Control, at a press conference on the steps of City Hall.

"Our concern is the public welfare of San Francisco and the integrity of its legislative processes. The tobacco companies' only concern is to sell more cigarets," he said.

The ordinance, which strictly limits smoking in the workplace, is a referendum item on the November ballot. The law says that if nonsmokers are not satisfied with an employer's efforts to accommodate smokers and nonsmokers, the employer must ban smoking in an office. Employers who fail to comply with the ordinance can be fined up to $500 a day.

The measure, written by Supervisor Wendy Nelder, was signed into law June 4 by Mayor Dianne Feinstein.

Critics who saw the ordinance as divisive, discriminatory and an example of government intrusion organized a drive to put the measure before the voters.

Supporters say the measure falls within the government's responsibility to pass laws protecting health and welfare. "It's the same as sanitation laws," said Weisberg.

The group hopes to raise about $100,000 for its campaign, he said.

The law would not be discriminatory or divisive, said Weisberg, a member of the national board of the American Cancer Society. "It's been done in many places," he said. "Nearly 60 percent of the population are non-smokers. What about discrimination against them in being exposed to harmful health effects."

Others were quick to point out the role of big tobacco companies in the fight to overturn the law.

"If the cigaret companies back on the East Coast hadn't decided to get this repealed, we wouldn't be standing here," said Stanton Glantz, an associate professor of medicine at the University of California's San Francisco Medical Center.

Florida's Theory on AIDS 'Dumping'

By Randy Shilts

The Florida health department said yesterday that fear among medical personnel of getting AIDS may have caused the curious transfer of an AIDS patient from Gainesville to San Francisco.

Morgan MacDonald, hospitalized for almost three months in Florida for treatment of acquired immune deficiency syndrome, was flown on a Learjet to San Francisco last Tuesday and placed on the office floor of the AIDS Founda-

opportunity within the law to avoid providing care," he said.

Pietrodangelo said the state government would take no action because "this was the action of one private hospital and did not in any way represent the policy of the state of Florida. This is an isolated instance."

Silverman said that he had heard of MacDonald's case even before the sick man arrived in San Francisco, because Florida social workers had contacted both the inpatient and out-patient facilities for

A week later, an ambulance pulled in front of the foundation's office on 10th Street and MacDonald was loaded on a gurney, pushed into the offices and deposited on the foundation's floor with a few plastic bags containing all his belongings.

"We were expecting a car or a cab, because they said he was ambulatory," said Power. "It was obvious from the start that he was real out of it. He couldn't even walk. The man needed hospitalization."

recuperative phase," according to Hunt, who said she participated in the discussions surrounding MacDonald's case. "He walked out of the hospital and he walked onto the plane."

Hunt said the social workers who arranged the flight were on vacation and not available for comment, but that they were "adamant" that they had told the truth to the San Francisco personnel.

"I'm in a quandary over all the controversy," she said. "His problems came from lying around a

Pumping had begun Friday evening after the Army Corps of Engineers granted a permit. Its issuance was opposed by sports fishermen and environmentalists on grounds that white bass could get past a newly built fish screen four miles above Tulare Lake and wreck the salmon and striped bass fisheries of the San Joaquin Sacramento river network.

The poisoning operation drew new criticism from the Kings County fishermen and also raised concerns about the possible threat to delta drinking water supplies.

"Fishing people are very much outraged," said Abel J. Meirelles of Hanford, the only member of the Kings County Board of Supervisors

the California Occupational Safety and Health Administration, said, "I don't think it's safe to give the fish away. They should be destroyed."

Greenberg said rotenone has been known to cause cancer in laboratory experiments with rats, although there has been no evidence of harmful effects on humans.

"They're putting poison into water that could go to the delta, which is a drinking water source for 15 million people," he said, "and no pumping should be allowed until not a trace of rotenone can be detected."

White said pumping would not be allowed to resume "until ...

Grodins

SAVE $36 ON OUR OWN RAMS HEAD VESTED SUITS

CORDUROY

$99

Our regular $135 pure cotton corduroy vested suits. They have a youthful fit and feature suede elbow patches, center vent and leather buttons. Regular, short and long sizes in chocolate, camel or charcoal. Pant cuffs free, charge for other alterations.

$22 BUTTON DOWNS Reg. 27.50 oxford cloth dress shirts in stripes and solid colors. $10 wool knit ties, $8.

$28 LAMBSWOOL V NECKS Reg. $35 full fashion saddle shoulder sweaters. In 6 great heather shades.

SAVE NOW FOR CAMPUS TIME

$25 FLANNEL PANTS Reg. 32.50 tri-blend washable flannel. Our own Rams Head label. Dressy solid colors.

$22 SHETLAND SWEATERS Reg. $30 Henri Savard full fashion, crew neck sweaters. Oatmeal, light grey, taupe, brown.

$109 SUEDE BOMBER Reg. $145 pigsuede zip-neck bomber by Tannery West. In grey, camel or black suede.

$38 FOGCUTTER JACKET Reg. $55 poly/cotton chintz jacket, dropped shoulders, zip-out hood. Black, tan, grey, navy.

33 stores to serve you, including Stockton/Market and Embarcadero

Retailer, maybe it's time to re-tailer your ads.

CHAPTER XII

VISIONS

Inspired by Christ, whose inspiration was from a higher authority, people have been receiving the most extraordinary visions ever since the great man awakened to his omniscient responsibility. Religious visions from the simplest to the most extravagant have been documented throughout history. Today miracle visions can be achieved by simply turning a knob: there is no idea, however miraculous, that cannot be created on a television screen.

You name it, TV can do it. The sea can be parted, the sky can fall, the world can dissolve to dust. The trouble is, TV tries too hard. The real miracle of television is its ability to transmit the simple, intimate, uncluttered idea, but nowhere is the extraordinary medium abused more than in the creation of television commercials.

A television location scout contacted me to arrange for the inspection of my house as a possible setting for a Pacific Telephone television commercial. Familiar with the outrageous extravagance typical of most TV commercial production, I consented to have the scout, the cameraman, the producer and their trailing entourage stop by and check out my digs. After three visits and much looking through fingers positioned at right angles to simulate a TV screen, they decided my house would be the perfect location in which to spend an entire day shooting the spot. In the interest of timeliness, I have updated the production costs to conform to the current budget standards for commercial production.

I suggested a fee of $5,000, a guarantee that they were insured for damage and breakage, and their promise to clean up when they were done. The fee was instantly accepted, causing me to wonder if it should have been $10,000 or more.

They showed me a storyboard of the commercial which blueprinted the scene that would occur in my house. It was a situation involving a medium shot of a movie producer chatting on the phone, plus a couple of other shots as he received a few party guests to view his new production on TV . Simple as that.

On the morning of the shoot, the entire street was thrown into a tizzy as sound trucks, generators, Winnebagos and other miscellaneous vehicles, including a catering truck, invaded the quiet residential neighborhood. Uniformed police provided traffic control and crowds of inquisitive and irate neighbors clustered in the street.

"What must they be filming, *Apocalypse II?* inquired a neighbor.

"It must be pretty big!" responded another.

A "production book" outlined the personnel who would be present in my living room, producing and supervising the few seconds of commercial film. There would be about forty people, not including the friends, hangers-on and gate crashers. From the client side would appear the advertising director and the public relations manager. From the advertising agency would be the producer, the art director, the copywriter, the account executive, the assistant account executive and the production coordinator. From the film production company would appear the director/cameraman, the key grip, someone designated as "best boy," the sound man, the makeup artist, the wardrobe mistress, the script person, the set director, the props person, the assistant props person, the VTR person, the production assistant, the driver, another driver and the caterer. Plus the principal actor and a few extras flown from Los Angeles to San Francisco to perform for a few seconds on film.

The functionaries responsible for this *sin*-ematographic event revealed to me that the production budget alone was "in the neighborhood of $150,000." Add to that the standard advertising agency production mark-up of 17.65 percent and you have an additional $26,475 overhead. Assuming a modest media budget of over one million to expose the commercial on the airwaves (the ad agency takes 15 percent to cover their presumed administrative and creative overhead) you can add yet an additional $150,000 to the cost of "creating" the commercial. Grand total for the 30 second epic, not including media costs: $326,475. Or $10,882.50 per second of film.

At that rate, a feature film for the theater/screen, which did not have any superstar costs or advertising/promotional costs built into the budget, would come in at over $58 million. That would be quite an elaborate movie, indeed.

I showed the Pacific Telephone TV storyboard to former ABC-TV executive producer Allen Paterson, a seasoned California film producer whose TV commercial clients include Chrysler Corporation, Del Monte Corporation, The Gap stores, Macy's, Knudsen Dairy Products and many more. I asked him for a production bid on the Pacific Telephone TV spot.

Considering all production costs to final answer print and including a healthy profit for his efforts, his bottom-line bid for the same commercial would be $25,000. A skillful freelance copywriter would have written the spot, or another equally persuasive, for $4,000. If Pacific Telephone were to have had an in-house agency, there would be no mark-ups or media commission costs. Hence, under different circumstances, that same commercial could have been produced for $29,000, a savings of $297,475. No wonder the Pacific Telesis Group has an annual media advertising budget of over $32 million. No wonder my telephone bills were so high last month.

But the numbing fact is that the Pacific telephone commercial production cost was typical. Far simpler commercials produced by the "prestige" film houses can come in at a much higher price.

Most television commercials go in one eye and out the other. Of those few that are memorable, most are remembered for their gimmickry. Indeed, it is often the gimmickry recalled instead of the product advertised. The viewer might say, "Oh, I just love that darling toilet paper commercial with the animals." But ask her which brand of toilet paper, and she won't remember.

Those channels booked wall-to-wall with commercials and promos will bombard you with hundreds of sales pitches in a single day. Those advertisers that have well-constructed commercials and that attack you with sufficient frequency stand a chance of getting their message across. Most of the rest fall on blind eyes and deaf ears.

In a typical week, the average viewer is exposed to some 650 television commercials alone, and perhaps 1,000 total advertising messages a day. The result of this torrent of advertising is viewer confusion: only 1.2 of the 650 TV ads seen each week can now be recalled. For ad professionals and advertisers that should be producing panic.

When you consider that a single exposure of a single 60-second TV spot can go for as much as $1,350,000 (a Superbowl spot), there are a lot of bucks going down the tube.

Procter & Gamble, which for years has been the leading exponent of the slice-of-life commercial, has contributed more to stultifying our senses than any advertiser in America. But those insufferable "Madges" chit-chatting over the back fence have sold a lot of detergent. Still, P & G would sell even more if they would rely less on the science of advertising and more on the art of persuasion.

The legendary salesman, Elmer Wheeler, used to say in his speeches to advertising clubs during the 1930s, "Don't sell the steak, sell the sizzle." This perverse wisdom has persuaded legions of copywriters to create TV commercials that do not effectively identify the product or its label. Instead, a bread commercial will dwell on insipid, unctuous children romping in a playground to illustrate energy (the "sizzle") and then tag the spot with a quick shot of the bread package (the "steak"). Viewers, dizzy from hours of jumpy, nervous television visuals, can hardly be expected to remember that particular brand of bread, the label of which was permitted only a few seconds on the screen.

The cosmetic industry inundates us with pretty ladies running in slow motion through fields of wild flowers, their dresses terpsichorating in the summer breeze, accompanied by a hundred

Mantovani-esque strings. It's enough to make you sick. But it's the client who should really be sickened because while the commercial is selling all that sizzle, his product and its label are hiding in the wings, lucky even to get a final bow.

While Lipton Tea may be well advised to simply sell the idea of tea drinking, since they'll get the lion's share of the business anyway, other products are not so privileged. Many minor products, bent on selling "sizzle," wind up selling their competitors' products more effectively than their own. The only commercial that I have seen to have effectively sold the "sizzle" is the national restaurant chain The Sizzler. The picture on the screen rarely leaves the product, a succulent, sizzling steak.

Who among us is not an armchair critic of TV commercials? But the *qualified* critic does not judge a commercial on whether or not he likes it, whether it is entertaining or not, whether it is offensive or inoffensive. The only criteria should be: is it remembered? does it persuade?

The *ideal* TV spot places the product in full view on the screen and leaves it there for the duration of the commercial. But who will sit still, staring at a bottle of Anacin or a box of Oxydol or a can of Fuller Paint when there is so much action to be found by turning the dial—or so much relief to be found by going to the bathroom?

One must admit that such a commercial would provide the optimum product identity, assuming that the viewer would view it. The enlightened writer of television commercials should start with just such a bare-bones premise. To come up with a brilliant selling concept within such narrow parameters is no easy task.

I have never attempted to write a television commercial without having a TV set near my typewriter, if only to stare at the blank screen and remind myself that the average TV picture is only about a foot high and a foot and a half wide. And viewed from across the room the picture gets smaller than that.

In the cloisters of their slick advertising offices, TV copywriters can forget they are writing pictures for this tiny, intimate medium. Sometimes their commercials are screened in large conference rooms, not on a TV monitor, but projected from a booth onto a theater screen. No wonder they so often stage productions that would make C.B. De Mille proud.

It was with these ideas in mind that I undertook an assignment to write a breakthrough commercial for Fuller Paint.

I placed a gallon of Fuller Paint in front of me on my desk. What to show? What to say? For years paint companies had been selling interior and exterior paint by talking about its maintenance characteristics—durability, washability, the like. But, I mused, that's not why people buy paint, especially for inside walls. They buy paint for the same reason they buy cosmetics—to beautify.

I studied the TV screen. I turned on the set, to be assailed by a frenzy of sights and sounds. I turned it off. I borrowed a grease pencil from an art director and drew a can of Fuller Paint on the TV tube, filling the entire screen with the identity of the product. "Now that's the way a TV commercial should look," I thought, "honest, forthright, direct, to the point."

But what to say? What to show? People are frightened of paint. Paint is formidable. Does not the suspicion of bad luck in walking under a ladder suggest that a paint can might fall on your head? Is not painting walls perceived as hard work? Does paint not drip on things, splatter your hair, stain your hands? How could I make Fuller Paint a friend, comforting, easy to apply, neat and clean—and beautiful? How could I accomplish all that and conjure a visual tour de force that would absolutely blow the competitors away?

My grease pencil drawing on my TV tube brought me back to earth. I had set my parameters. The can would not budge from the screen. At least when my Fuller Paint commercial was over, the viewer would not mistake the message as being from Sherwin-Williams or DuPont, or, for that matter, another product category entirely.

I got a screwdriver and pried open the lid of the can. The paint was the whitest I'd ever seen. I tilted the can just a tad. Like undulating marshmallows. Not just beautiful, but sensual. Had anyone ever really *seen* paint before? Not on the TV screen they hadn't. Paint had always been seen as a can or being rolled or slapdashed onto a wall. No one had ever *really* seen paint before, not as I was seeing it then. I was actually *feeling* the paint. Feeling the paint? I rolled up my sleeve and plunged my hand into the can. The paint squished through my fingers, cool and soft, almost obscenely delicious to feel. Then in walked my secretary.

"Have you totally lost your mind?" she inquired.

"I've just found it, thank you!"

I plunged my other hand into the can and withdrew clasped fists with the paint squeezing, oozing through the openings between my fingers. Marilyn watched, slack-jawed, spoon-bottom eyes disbelieving, fascinated, wondering what it was all about.

"I need more paint. Get me red, blue, green. Get me magenta!"

She sensed the urgency of my need and dashed for the petty cash and out the door for the closest Fuller Paint store.

I lined up all five open cans before me. Red screamed out to me, "Let me warm you up!" Green screamed out, "Let me cool you off!" Magenta beckoned, "Let me excite you!"

My hand plunged first into white and then into red. The two colors dripped like liquid marble through my tightening fist. And then into blue. A liquid flag creamed down my fingers. Magenta was next. And when my hand surfaced it was crawling with gorgeous colors, each blending with the others. I raised my hand and lifted it above the mouth of the can. I turned my hand at a right angle and watched the awesome Niagara of colors pour down.

"Goddamn, that's fantastic," I screamed in triumph. "Get me some illustration board! Hurry!"

Marilyn placed a clean white sheet on the desk top next to the open cans. With one stroke, my pigmented palm painted a rainbow across the board. "My god, it goes on so smooth and easy you don't even need a brush!"

Had I just conceived the perfect television commercial? In my mind I had, because the product and its identifying label need never leave the screen. Was there relevancy? Of course, because the commercial would be dramatizing color and beauty and sensuality—the *real* reasons people buy interior paint, not for durability, washability and other janitorial advantages. Would the commercial hold attention? (Was Stalin a Communist?) Would Fuller Paint emerge as a friend, not to be feared? I figured a hand making love to paint could dispel all such fears. And, finally, would the commercial dramatize how simple and easy Fuller was to apply and clean up? A paint-soaked hand actually applying the paint and effortlessly cleansed under a water tap would prove all that, too. I was absolutely sold. Now to sell the client!

This commercial was concocted shortly after western Fuller Paint Company was purchased by the eastern paint company, O'Brien, to become Fuller-O'Brien Corporation. It would be necessary that I persuade a great many corporate executives on the wisdom of the idea. Rather than rely on scripts or storyboards, I elected to perform the concept live, in as many offices and conference rooms as necessary, until final approval for film production was obtained.

I knew the concept would have the support of Fuller's adventuresome young advertising manager, Carl Makela. However, Jerry Gibbons had some concern about the president of O'Brien Paint, Jerry Crowley, newly responsible for Fuller Paint, too, who had him worried. Many of the executives whose authority fell somewhere between the ad manager and the president preferred to take a wait-and-see attitude.

On the occasion of my presentation to the executive staff in the Fuller conference room, Mr. Crowley was the last to arrive. Jerry began the presentation with a chart, knowing how comforting charts can be to the corporate mentality. Charts at once suggest ordered thinking, rational planning. Aware of my reputation as a crazy, I needed all the ammunition that could be mustered. The chart underscored various marketing objectives and highlighted such concerns as impact and demographics.

The dour Mr. Crowley shook his head laterally, as if to say no, to every point made. The chart presentation completed, I introduced five gallon cans of Fuller Paint to the conference table. "Gentlemen, I'm going to give you a live presentation of this commercial and I'd like to mention that the voice we are recommending to deliver it is the haunting voice of Mr. Ken Nordine," who, I reminded them, delivered the famed Fuller Paint radio commercials a number of years back.

Mr. No-No shook his head.

"The narrator's voice," I continued, "will be underscored with light rhythms and supportive musical effects."

I pried the lids from the cans, removed my coat and rolled up my shirt sleeve. I plunged my hand into the first color and began the narration:

> Dr. Freud might have had something to say about this paint. [Bright red oozed through my fingers.]
>
> There's something about the way it pours and flows and undulates. [I dipped in for more paint and let it flow from my cupped hand.] And goes on so smooth and easy—you almost don't need a brush. [I painted the surface of an illustration board with my paint-soaked palm.]
>
> Your walls are very personal things. They surround you and

protect you. [Hand plunged into next can, which contained orange.] And covered with color they can warm you up. [Hand into next can, green.] Or cool you off. [Hand into magenta.] Or excite you!

[Hand moves to white paint and rainbow pours from fist.] Fuller believes paint is very personal, and with over a thousand colors there's a Fuller color just for you. [I dipped randomly into the various cans, letting the colors blend and fuse.] Fuller Paint, since 1849, painting the colorful West—the best.

In a theatrical setting one would reasonably expect applause to follow such a performance. In the hallowed chambers of the Fuller conference room I at least expected *some* reaction. The executive staff surrounding Mr. Crowley eyed each other, careful not to betray a reaction or give a clue as to whether they liked it or not. They would wait first for Mr. Crowley to respond.

I broke the self-conscious silence myself. "Well, what do you think?"

Mr. Crowley shook his head, not in wide negative movements, but in short, staccato jerks as if to say, "Tsk, tsk, shame on you."

Jerry handed me a roll of paper towels to wipe my hand. "This commercial, skillfully produced, with very sensitive pacing and soft lap dissolves, can have a major impact on the market place," I said.

But my confidence was waning. Mr. Crowley kept shaking his head left and right.

"Well, what do you think, Mr. Crowley?" I implored.

"What do you think?" the president asked his marketing director.

"What do you think?" the marketing director asked the product manager.

"Well, it certainly is different," he said, noncommittally.

Mr. Crowley stood. For the first time his head stopped shaking. "I think it's perfect," he said.

The conference table erupted into lively conversation, almost a celebration. Mr. Crowley was all smiles, his head still shaking no-no.

"Why does he always shake his head?" I whispered to Jerry.

"Just a little nervous tic," he answered.

You've learned enough about creating television advertising by now. It's time for your quiz. I want you to cook up four television ideas for four entirely different product/service categories. I will give you the marketing problem. Then you will put on your creative thinking cap and come up with a snappy TV commercial idea that solves the problem.

Your clients will be European Health Spas, once America's largest chain of health clubs and gyms; Marine World—Africa USA, a northern California theme/amusement park; the Sierra Club, America's largest and most influential conservation organization; and Bay View Federal Savings, a large California savings and loan.

After you have created in your mind's eye and ear each marvelous commercial, I will then present for your judgment the commercial that I created to solve the particular marketing problem. Using my commercial as a benchmark, you may then give yourself a grade. You may grade me also, if you wish. Do not be afraid to flunk yourself. Nor need you have any compunction about flunking me, either.

For each of the four assignments I will ask you to develop a theme line or slogan that will be applicable to other advertising media. So, in a sense you will be creating not just a single television commercial, but a concept for an entire campaign. Remember, the most effective TV commercial is staged in close-up, the camera focusing on the product. In the case of the Sierra Club and European Health Spas, there is no product per se, so your message must focus on a central "idea" that you conclude will solve the client's problems or take advantage of the client's opportunities. Because we are on the honor system, if your commercial ideas are boring or if the pictures on the TV screen are irrelevant, I will expect you to flunk yourself.

EUROPEAN HEALTH SPAS MARKETING PROBLEM/OPPORTUNITY

By today's spending standards, this huge national chain will spend over $20 million annually on advertising. Competition is getting tougher, with second-rate spas springing up all over the place, cutting prices and offering premiums, deals, gimmicks, and come-ons. Everyone's ads and commercials are pretty much the same—el schlocko! They all feature the same themes—physical fitness, health, and price advantage. The principal concern of all spa advertising is to get telephone leads. European Health Spas wishes to increase its leads and establish itself as special and different—*the* distinguished name in health spas.

(This blank space is provided so that you may mull over the problem and come up with an idea.)

Your time's up. Here's the Pritikin solution: I kept thinking, Why do people go to health spas? One could logically conclude: for their health. That, I questioned. While health spa members would be the first to attribute their motivation to health and physical fitness, perhaps their real reasons are more related to vanity, making themselves more attractive to the opposite sex, by shedding weight, toning their muscles—in a word, looking sexier. I envisaged a kind of body ballet, the camera up so close that in some scenes the viewer would not orient to which parts of the body were in motion. The motion would be slow and graceful and fluid, flowing with a soft melodic line. Cranked up to achieve slow motion, the camera would train its lens on naked flesh, undulating, exercising, gently twisting and turning to the rhythms of a full string section. Underwater cameras would study aquatic exercise in bubbling pools. Biceps, swelling from working pulley weights, would add muscle to the message. Pretty girls would exhilarate in the marvelous tonic of exercise. To insure "product" identification, the camera would spend a great deal of time on chests and midsections. On the tank tops of the men, the words *European Health Spas* would be very visible; and the women, in their leotards and body stockings, would also display the European Health Spas logotype.

Now, for a slogan, one that would set well to music, look great on a T-shirt, arrest attention in a newspaper ad, provoke excitement on radio, function on an outdoor billboard. It should be sexy but dignified, sell-worthy and sensual. Perhaps it should even qualify as a bumper sticker, the ultimate free medium. The answer, as usual, came in a flash—maybe it came in a flesh:

I WANT YOUR BODY

Lissa Sumner, the spas' pawky advertising manager, heard the slogan once and screamed with delight. "Let's do it, do it, do it!" she cried. Instantly she engaged the full amount of her not-too-shabby resources and the campaign was off and running.

Here is the script of the television commercial:

(THE VIDEO PORTION IS A CONTINUUM OF SOFT OPTICAL DISSOLVES FEATURING A WELL-BUILT MAN AND WOMAN ENGAGED IN EXERCISE, WITH SPECIAL ATTENTION TO THE LEOTARDS AND TANK TOPS, WHICH DISPLAY "EUROPEAN HEALTH SPAS." FLASHES OF CHROME WEIGHTS, PULLEYS, AND MODERN EXERCISE EQUIPMENT GIVE DAZZLING VISUAL PUNCTUATIONS AND DESCRIBE THE STATE-OF THE ART FACILITIES. THE EXERCISE MOVEMENTS ARESHOT IN SLOW MOTION AND CUT TO PRECISE SYNC WITH THE RICH, RHYTHMIC INSTRUMENTAL BACKGROUND.)

GIRL SINGING (OFF CAM): I want your body.
ANNOUNCER (OFF CAM): Phone 824-9940.

(SUPERIMPOSE OVER SCENE THE PHONE NUMBER.)

BOY SINGING (OFF CAM): I want your body.
ANNOUNCER (OFF CAM): 824-9940.
BOTH SINGING: I want your body.
ANNOUNCER (OFF CAM): 824-9940.
BOTH SINGING: And I want it now.

(LUSCIOUS SCENES FOLLOW AS THE VELVET-VOICED ANNOUNCER INTONES HIS NARRATIVE.)

ANNOUNCER: I want your body at the European Health Spas—to be exercised and pampered to a new vitality. I want your body to have nutrition...the beauty that once it had...to have tone and trim muscularity. I want your body to visit the world's largest and most prestigious organization of health clubs, European Health Spas.
BOTH SINGERS: I want your body now.

(SUPERIMPOSE PHONE NUMBER AND LOGO OVER FINAL SCENES.)

ANNOUNCER: Your first trial visit free. 824-9940.

Over a period of some thirty months, the European Health Spas put the equivalent of $40 million behind the campaign, generating tens of millions of dollars in new business for their 150 spas around the United States. In retrospect, I have but one regret. During the casting call in San Francisco for the female lead of the thirty-second commercial, we studied some fifty models and fledgling actresses. One in particular, an early reject because she was too "hippy," too "clumsy," and too "self-conscious," unfolded a few years later as the star of a major TV series and a photo spread in *Playboy*—Suzanne Somers.

MARINE WORLD—AFRICA USA MARKETING PROBLEM/OPPORTUNITY

Marine World, an out-sized aquarium on the San Francisco Peninsula which features trained dolphins and a couple of killer whales, is losing money. The attraction is bought by Resorts International, a Bahamanian conglomerate, which commits a few million dollars to improving the operation and signed on Ralph Helfer, a Hollywood wild animal trainer, to add some blood-and-guts to the otherwise tepid aquatic attraction. Ralph appears on the scene with a full zoo of hippos, harpy eagles and assorted beasties, proclaiming "affection training." While the Resorts International management prefers a theme of "terror," the gentle Ralph Helfer prevails with his philosophy about tigers, lions, tarantulas and deadly snakes, saying, "If you love them, they will love you." He refers constantly to Charlie, his famed cougar of the Mercury commercials, who would eat, not your hand, but out of it.

Ralph wins, and so the advertising campaign parameters are drawn. The principal medium will be television and the theme "affection training" will permeate all media in the area. Marine World, with its marvelous ichthyological wonders and aquatic mammalians, will blend with Africa USA to encompass the terrors of the jungle and to create a dazzling new attraction—whose break-even point will be a gross of some $7 million in revenue during a five-month season.

You, my reader, are now engaged to come up with the TV commercial, which in sixty seconds, as well as in a condensed thirty-second version, will translate all this marvelousness to the ever-consuming public through the scanlines and pixels of their TV screens. Your central TV theme or slogan, I should remind you, should also function in newspaper ads, radio, outdoor billboards, bumper stickers and even promotional hypes with regional and local advertising tie-ins, not excluding paper-napkin imprints at McDonald's.

(This blank space is provided so that you may mull over the problem and come up with an idea.)

Your time's up. Here's the Pritikin solution: I pictured in my mind's eye and ear a veritable garden of Eden where creatures of the jungle and creatures of the sea would be living together in harmony. It would be wild, but not in the bestial sense. It would be absolutely wild in the idiomatic sense—far-out, implausible, impossible to believe without seeing it for yourself.

The television camera would capture the grace and beauty of the affection-trained beasts interrelating with humans and species other than their own in a gentle spirit never imagined possible outside of an animated Disney film. The lion would lie down with the lamb; the tiger would walk freely through crowds of adoring children; the llama would bat its lashes; the camel would kiss the lens; the killer whale would kill you with kindness. I would write a song to express the poetry of this extraordinary new attraction and it would be sung with a sweet, tender respect for all living creatures.

While television would be the principal medium, a single theme, expressed in a few simple words, would report the news of this oasis of love in multimedia print advertising. Without actually saying "new," the theme would quickly telegraph that something very special had happened at Marine World:

MARINE WORLD GOES WILD!

As you read the audio portion of the television commercial, let your imagination plug in the video. I should mention that this sixty-second picture-poem included thirty-three separate scenes, each edited in perfect sync to the soft rhythms of the music.

MARINE WORLD
"LION WITH THE LAMB"
60 SEC TV AUDIO TRACK

SINGERS: There is a place, where the lion lies with the lamb.
The tiger and the killer whale, swim free.
Creatures of the jungle, and creatures of the sea,
Living together in harmony.
It's called Marine World, Marine World.
It's absolutely wild.

ANNOUNCER: Six hundred jungle beasts have been affection-trained to live in open space uncaged with Marine World's life of the sea. And you will go among them on a sea safari so astonishing, so marvelous that your mind will barely believe what your eyes will see. Now Africa USA has joined Marine World and there is nothing else like it in the world today. Only minutes south of the San Francisco Airport. It is absolutely wild

SINGERS: Marine World, Marine World.
It's absolutely wild.

The record crowds for opening week were absolutely wild. Attendance didn't climb, it leaped. By the end of the season, attendance more than doubled over the previous year, guaranteeing the continuing, burgeoning success of this once-failing attraction.

A curious addendum to this corporate success reminds me of an individual success equally wild. A number of years before my involvement with Marine World, I had a pleasant brush with the Ice Follies. I recall having less than two hours notice to prepare a new business pitch to this famed attraction. It was one of those days where there was literally nobody in the advertising agency except a few secretaries and a young mailboy/trainee type, a certain Mike Demetrios, who wore tweedy suits and was reputed to have an M.B.A. from Harvard. "Mike," I said, "I want you to participate in this presentation. You will be perceived as an account executive. Please look terribly concerned and studious, say as little as possible, and take a lot of notes."

The prospective client was adequately persuaded with my pyrotechnics and sufficiently convinced of Mike's quiet power to award my agency the coveted account. Soon thereafter, Mike bloomed with such inordinate speed that he was hired away from the ad agency and given a job in the marketing department of Ice Follies. While the chronology of events thereafter is somewhat blurred in my memory, the relevant fact is that Mike was later snatched from Ice Follies for a better job at Marine World as vice president and manager of the park.

No longer my mailboy/trainee, he was now my client. I'll never forget the day the letter arrived. It was a nice letter, courteous and corporate in its tone, but the bottom line was clear: "You're fired."

There are sometimes curious and obscure reasons people or companies are fired. Top management, with its presumed powers, is often the most supplicatory, answering sometimes to almost invisible higher authorities. For Mike Demetrios, I suspect, there was a Wizard of Oz, intoning directives from the far-away Bahamas. With Marriott's Great America opening a major theme park down the road a piece, Mike was especially sensitive to Bahamanian demands for big changes fast. And so—the Dear John letter. Such decisions are very much a part of corporate life. And political life, too, where a single human soul can be divested of his job because—well, just because.

Today Mike is no longer the general manager. He is the president and principal owner of the huge attraction. He must be getting very rich. I wish him continued success. I trust he will reflect on those early wild campaigns that turned the park around, and the warm letter which Marine World sent Jerry Gibbons and me years after we were fired. It was on the eve of Marine World's tenth anniversary. It said thanks for those wild campaigns and added that without them there never would have been a tenth anniversary. Mike, you tiger you.

THE SIERRA CLUB MARKETING PROBLEM/OPPORTUNITY

America's largest and most influential conservation organization, with an active paid membership of some 493,000 concerned citizens, wishes to make a statement on television about saving energy. If the statement has *any* political overtones, the club, because of its tax-exempt nonpolitical status, will have to pay for the television time to air the commercial. If the message is sufficiently generic in its appeal, they stand a chance of getting free air time, known in the business as "PSs" or Public Service Spots.

Jim Belsey, a rumpled, tweedy, craggy guy with twinkly eyes and boundless loyalty to the cause, appears in my office in a cloud of cigarette smoke. He is the Sierra Club's paid PR/advertising rep. His arms are filled with books and memos and government reports delineating the cause and scope of the crisis. Because this is your test, not mine, I herewith hand you from the pages of this book an imaginary sheaf of data. You will read about BTU's; you will see graphs describing thermal waste; you will learn all you need know about oil, gas and electricity. You may discover, as I did, that the problems with oil are caused by the oily profiteers, what's happening to natural gas is a laughing gas, and the deplorable drain on our electrical resources is a shocker. But in your TV commercial you must not dare touch on those sensitive areas lest you get political and lose your PS advantage.

You now have the opportunity to develop a unique persuasion, send a clarion call to your fellow Americans to sacrifice in the name of patriotism, and appeal to their consciences to save energy, with all its implications of reducing inflation, ending dependency on foreign powers, and perhaps leaving a few barrels of fuel in the ground for some succeeding generation.

(This blank space is provided so that you may mull over the problem and come up with an idea.)

Your time's up. Here's the Pritikin solution: I thought first of God, country, and family, a return to patriotism where a nation battles against an insufferable foe. Could not the American people fight the energy war with the same fervor and zeal the doughboys mustered in World War I? Was not this, too, a battle for survival, independence and freedom? It was. But my plan would never work. No less an actor than Ronald Reagan had just stood before the TV cameras with the same jingoistic appeal. And it fell on deaf national ears as he needlessly burned a trillion electro-kilowatts on TV screens across the land.

My plan would appeal not to the heart strings but to the purse strings. I wondered how much cold cash the average family could save by engaging the simplest procedures to conserve energy. Suppose they cut down their driving, turned down the heat, turned off a few lights? My calculations demonstrated that the average small family could effortlessly save $500 each year. The theme line for this sixty-second and thirty-second TV commercial, with applications for other uses, would be:

SAVE ENERGY—
WE'LL ALL BE THE RICHER FOR IT.

Sadly, my first visual concept came a cropper because of our nitpicking U.S. Treasury Department. It was my plan simply to light a match to a $500 bill. As the viewer breathlessly watched this painful demonstration, an announcer's voice would explain how the average family needlessly burns up at least $500 in energy each year. The clincher would come at the end with the camera held on the shriveled, smoldering, ashen, non-negotiable $500 bill. The announcer would then explain how that $500 could be saved. By running the film backward, the flame would reappear, crawling across the fragile, blackened currency, inch-by-inch restoring the money to its original crisp $500 bill. A hand would present the bill to the viewer and state, "Here, take it, it's yours—if you'll just save on energy."

The argument that removing $500 from the economy would help ease inflation, however slightly, did not persuade the unbudgeable Treasury Department to relax its policy on destroying money. I therefore created another visual, to be videotaped, not filmed, so as to conform to yet another Treasury Department policy.

Because the real subject was *money,* not *energy,* the TV screen would feature money. Two male hands in tight close-up would grip a wad of moolah, including a couple of hundred-dollar bills, a fifty, twenties, tens and fives. The hands would beckon the viewer to take the money and, in fact, hand the currency to the lens of the camera. As the hand would withdraw the money would be gone, presumably taken by an unseen viewer. This appeal to avarice, instead of patriotism, would be supported with a taut, tense, music/effects underpinning, and the announcer's voice would have an urging authority as it beseeched the viewer to "Take it, here take it, it's yours!"

Here, then, is the narrator's copy. As you read it, glance at the screen of your television set and just imagine the dramatic impact and persuasion this mini-drama evoked:

SIERRA CLUB
60 SECOND TV

ANNOUNCER: Here...here's a hundred dollars for you. Go on—take it. Do you drive a car? Here—you can get another hundred. Go on. Tell you what. If you stop burning those lights you don't need, take another fifty. Most of us are

```
burning money—by burning up energy
wastefully. You might as well have
it in cold cash. Put on a sweater and
turn down the heat. That's probably
worth another fifty. At least. Put
in insulation and you put money in
the bank. Could be worth a hundred
a year—or a lot more. Oh, go on—take
it all. It's tax free. Five hundred
dollars. That's how much the average
family can save in just one year if
they'll just cut down on the gas, oil
and electricity they burn up for no
purpose. It really pays to conserve
energy. We'll all be the richer for
it.

SUPERIMPOSE SLOGAN OVER VIDEO:
   SAVE ENERGY. WE'LL ALL BE RICHER FOR IT.
```

It would be very difficult to determine the success or failure of the energy spot, except subjectively. However, it's nice to know that its persuasion on television has been augmented by its exposure in yet another medium—this book. I trust you will respond by putting on a sweater and turning down the heat.

BAY VIEW FEDERAL SAVINGS MARKETING PROBLEM/OPPORTUNITY

Bay View Federal Savings & Loan, among California's biggest, with assets over $2 billion, is in deep trouble. So are many of the other S&Ls. Bay View is thinking of slashing its million dollar per year advertising budget and laying low until the money market crisis blows over.

Elwood Hanson, Bay View's feisty board chairman, decided to go for broke. He wants a blockbuster advertising campaign that will salvage his losses, build his share of market, devastate his competitors and, not at all sanctimoniously, provide an informational service to Californians bewildered about the national economy and frightened about their own personal financial lives.

Historically, Bay View has advertised its various "instruments" in newspapers, headlining, along with the rest, this week's new high interest on such-and-such an account. If you will leaf through almost any daily newspaper, you will be inundated with S&L advertising screaming in typographical frenzy the latest high yield on this or that account. Rarely is a substantive competitive advantage ever expressed and each ad is so muddled with asterisks, qualifiers, tiny type and government mandatories, that even if one S&L *had* a competitive edge, it would be difficult to ferret it out.

Here are a few headlines gleaned from ads pushing Treasury Bill Certificates during that time in recent American history when the annual inflation rate was actually higher than the highest yields offered on savings accounts.

For Foothill Thrift:
FOOTHILL PAYS MORE,
12% THRIFT CERTIFICATES EQUALS 12.75% ANNUAL YIELD

For Allstate Savings:
NOT JUST A PRETTY RATE,
14.956% ANNUALIZED YIELD 15.72%

For Gibraltar Savings:
HIGHEST INTEREST FOR ALL SAVINGS,
10.4% ANNUAL YIELD 11.2%

For American Savings:
NOW $5,000 OPENS A $10,000 ACCOUNT,
14.956% ANNUAL YIELD 15.742%

For World Savings:
LATEST MONEY MARKET RATE,
11.858% ANNUALIZED YIELD 12.43%

The text of each of the ads provides the necessary ifs, ands and buts, so that it eventually becomes clear to the reader that a higher interest rate requires a longer saving commitment or some other type of penalty. So in fact all savings and loan organizations at a given time are offering and advertising pretty much identical opportunities.

Bay View has decided to shift from print to television. In thirty seconds they wish to pre-empt all of their competitors with a new approach, one that will establish their leadership in the industry and, of course, conform to the myriad laws imposed by the regulatory agencies that watchdog the industry.

Put on your thinking cap and come up with a breathtaking and persuasive TV commercial that will translate into other media as well.

(This blank space is provided so that you may mull over the problem and come up with an idea.)

Your time's up. Here's the Pritikin solution: The dizzying experience of studying the competitors' ads and watching their TV commercials taught me all I had to know about what *not* to do. In much of the advertising, I sensed an essential dishonesty. Not false claims, not half-truths, not bait-and-switch, not that kind of dishonesty but rather a convolution of the facts about savings and interest-earning in America. The pervasive thrust was "You earn more" at such and such; or "The highest interest in the land," or "Turn $5,000 into $10,000."

I questioned the essential honesty of such advertising. Because in the pre-Reagan Year of our Lord 1980, no one earned at a bank or a savings and loan. With the national inflation rate soaring about 18 percent and in the northern California Bay Area in March of 1980 up to 30 percent, including housing, how in hell could a depositor "earn" when the highest interest rate allowed by federal law fell far short of the rate of inflation?

Could not my new campaign for Bay View penetrate the morass of S&L hoopla with a disarming respect for the depositor who certainly knew the facts of life about interest and inflation? Could not my new campaign, heralded by a single TV commercial, jolt the entire S&L industry into a new reality and reach the prospective depositor with such stunning impact that, all factors being equal, he would choose Bay View Federal Savings as the definitive, trusted institution for keeping his money secure—and, at the very least, provide interest as high as or higher than he would get elsewhere? If honesty *is* the best policy, why not just tell it like it is?

YOU LOSE LESS AT BAY VIEW

I wanted the thirty-second TV commercial to reach out of the tube and shake the viewer into a new awareness, a new trust in advertising, and a very special confidence in the one savings and loan institution that would dare discuss, openly and honestly, the unprecedented dilemma of saving money in America in 1980. I also was beginning to taste the marvelous PR opportunities of such a campaign.

My spokesman would be Uncle Sam. The commercial would open on a medium shot of the nation's beleaguered uncle with a wad of money in his hand. The music in the background would be wrenching in its strident, melancholy theme: It would be a single piano, droning slowly in flatted chords, the otherwise rousing "Battle Hymn of the Republic." I remembered Barbra Streisand's

"Happy Days Are Here Again" sung with such sadness and despair. The instrumental background for the Bay View spot would hit the same mournful, joyless note.

As the camera moved in to study the face of Uncle Sam, he would deliver his message. "Inflation," he would bemoan, "what a crying shame." And as the camera would pause for a lingering moment, his eyes would glisten with sadness. He would address the viewer with his message about saving money, about Bay View's concern, and he would invite the viewer to consider Bay View as a resource to plan for the future. And, to achieve the ultimate thirty-second drama, a quiet tear would fall over his craggy cheek. Glory, indeed—glory, GLORY Hallelujah!

Last year Americans spent more than 275 billion, 18 million hours watching television. The statistics of television can be as staggering as its content can be suffocating. Most American children have spent more time in front of a television set by the end of high school than they have inside of a classroom. During an average day, over 75 percent of us watch; during a week, 90 percent. Last year, upwards of $15 billion was spent in the purchase of TV sets, many billions forked out by families who desired a second or third set for the bedroom or bathroom. Heavens, there are some who, when nature calls, wouldn't dare miss even a commercial.

The time spent watching the boob tube approximates the time spent with radio, newspapers and magazines combined. It is probable that more time is spent watching TV in the U.S. than any other single human activity. This socio-cultural revolution is made possible primarily through over 1,053 commercial television stations and has been brought to you by such benefactors as McDonald's Egg McMuffin, Advil's advanced remedy for pain,

New Morning Fresh, Snuggies. Plus countless more products and services that have underwritten a new way of life for us and the rest of the world.

Today, you are among the few who are reading words in a book instead of watching a flickering picture on a TV tube. If you are reading this book at prime time instead of watching the *Cosby Show, L.A. Law, Thirty-something, Roseanne, Murphy Brown, Dallas,* or *Nova,* you are a rare bird indeed. Because, between 8 P.M. and 11 P.M. 88 million Americans forsake reading words for watching pictures. Some of these pictures, including, and perhaps especially, the commercials, can be mighty marvelous. But still, let us all pray.

EPILOGUE

REVELATIONS

What if Jesus had been born in your generation instead of the year one, and in Brooklyn instead of Bethlehem? And what if his father, Joseph, were a copywriter instead of a carpenter?

"Hello," he might say to the receptionist at BREA&D advertising agency. "My name is Jesus Christ. I'm interested in a job with your creative department."

"Please have a seat, Mr. Christ. I'll call Personnel."

He would sit in the stylish reception room and study the ads on the walls. Whatever would he think, this burgeoning genius, this man of such complex simplicity, this honest man who cherished truth more than life itself, this simple soul dressed in common clothes, this man who would be nailed to a Cross to defend what he believed?

He picked up a magazine and started flipping through it. The headlines on the cigarette ads, created just before the U.S. cracked down on the shameful industry, leaped out at him:

DORAL II
NO OTHER CIGARETTE
WITH THIS LITTLE TAR

NOW WINS—2 MG TAR

CARLTON LOWEST—0.5 MG TAR

How could all three claim to be lowest in tar when each had a different tar content? He checked the Doral II ad again: NO OTHER CIGARETTE WITH THIS LITTLE TAR... He discovered the trick at the bottom of the page....HAS THIS MUCH TASTE. He looked at the Now ad, which showed a Now package standing triumphantly on top of Carlton. How could this be when Now had 2 mg of tar and Carlton had only 0.5? NOW WINS, he read again, and then saw the subhead: OF THE TWO LOWEST TAR BRANDS, TESTS PROVE NOW IS MORE SATISFYING. A bit spurious, he thought. He looked at the Carlton ad, which featured a chart comparing Carlton's tar content with that of its competitors. Doral II and Now weren't even on the list, although other brands with far higher tar content were. Plainly, because Doral II and Now were Carlton's closest competitors, Carlton chose simply not to list them. "That's simply not honest," thought the honest man.

He picked up another popular magazine. On the back cover was a full color ad for Kent Golden Lights 100. He turned the pages, reading from back to front as so many people do. A sweet-looking lady looked out at him from an advertisement. The headline, in bold reverse type, screamed

BLOW YOUR LOVER

It continued on a second line, UP TO 8" x 10" IN FULL COLOR. The text of the copy continued, "All photos accepted—privacy guaranteed. Full size color copies on Kodak finish paper." "Jesus Christ!" he mumbled all too audibly.

"Personnel can't see you today," the receptionist announced. "But Mr. Judas Iscariot can give you a few minutes. He's the account executive on the Buferoon account."

Seated in Iscariot's office, Jesus was asked, "Have you any experience in advertising?"

"No, sir, but I feel I understand human nature. And I think if advertising were more honest, it would work better."

"Look," Iscariot said, "I don't want to discourage you, but have you thought of going into religion."

"Perhaps you might try me on an assignment. Maybe an advertising problem your people can't solve."

Iscariot rolled his eyes. "You think if our creative people couldn't solve an advertising problem that you could?"

"Perhaps," Jesus said, "I could try my hand at a Buferoon ad. It's my understanding that the client is thinking about shopping around for another agency."

"How in heaven's name did you hear that?"

Iscariot was well aware that BREA&D was on notice from Buferoon, but how could this confidential information have hit the street? The agency was already furiously preparing new campaigns to try to hang on to the multimillion-dollar account. So secret were the preparations that copywriters and art directors had holed up in an obscure hotel, working day and night to save the account. A guard was stationed outside the door to ensure that no copy or layouts left the room.

"Mr. Christ, I can assure you that account has never been more secure with us, but if you want to make a stab at an ad, here's a client file. No confidential information, but a lot of secondary data on the analgesic market, demographics, competitors. If you get any ideas, come back and we'll run 'em up the flagpole."

Later Jesus went through the file. The collection of competitive ads were, for the most part, peas in one conventional pod. There was a "me-too-ism" in the look and thrust of the ads. In many, the competitive products were displayed in the background as the headline and copy attempted to weasel some advantage, however, vague or confusing, for the foreground product. He looked at the medical background. There was no medical concensus that a buffered aspirin like Buferoon reached the pain significantly faster than plain aspirin.

He tugged on his beard and his eyes looked to the heavens, as eyes so often do when they search for an answer. And suddenly, in a flash, he had the answer. He would try honesty. "Could it be," he thought, "that honesty is the best gimmick" Honesty so unremitting, so unrelenting, so penetrating, so persuasive that even the most jaded disbeliever would have to be convinced. Pure, unadulterated, unfiltered, undiluted, understated, overwhelming honesty!" Jesus knew he had a hot idea.

What an advertising breakthrough he would create! Buferoon would say to all the world, BUY BAYER ASPIRIN—IT'S A NICE PRODUCT, TOO. Buferoon would be the first to make such a Christian gesture to its foe in the marketplace. Jesus would write a nice and humble campaign for Buferoon. He scrawled the ad on a piece of paper.

A KIND WORD ABOUT BAYER ASPIRIN FROM THE MAKERS OF BUFEROON

We are sorry if our advertising for Buferoon may have given you a headache. Maybe you should take a Bayer Aspirin. After all—our pain relievers are exactly the same, 5 grains of salicylic acid.

For years we have said, "More doctors recommend the pain reliever in Buferoon." While it's true, we hope now that it was not deceptive. Because our pain reliever is plain aspirin. Nothing more, nothing less. It's always been on our label—in small print.

Now—what about our buffering ingredient? While doctors agree that our tablet physically dissolves faster in the stomach than a nonbuffered aspirin—there is some dispute about whether our pain reliever gets to the pain any faster than plain aspirin without the buffering compound.

What then is the advantage of a Buferoon? For those people who might get a tummy upset from aspirin alone, our buffering additive (aluminum glycinate and magnesium carbonate) should help soothe the problem.

One more thing: You're going to love our new TV commercials—especially if you have a headache. We're going to show beautiful pastoral scenes, bubbling brooks, fields of daisies, that sort of thing, and the music will be soft and gentle. Just in case you have a headache when our commercial comes on—the pretty pictures and soft music will help soothe you. If that doesn't work—take a Buferoon. Or a Bayer Aspirin. Bayer makes a good product, too.

BUFEROON
HONEST—IT WORKS

"Did you come up with a winner?" Iscariot asked as Christ handed him the ad the next day. He quickly scanned the copy. "Incredible," he mumbled. "Absolutely unbelievable." He raised his eyes briefly to study Jesus. "It's astonishing you think this would ever sell to the client. However, I will say it's a new slant. Whose side are you on, anyway—ours or Bayer's?"

"Neither," said Jesus. "It seems to me the sufferer with a headache is entitled to the honest facts."

"O.K.," Iscariot said. "Check back in a few days."

The main conference room was readied. The massive conference table was arranged with the precision of a Tish Baldridge table setting. At each seat was a fresh yellow pad, a pencil so pointy it looked like a weapon, a cup and saucer and a package of gum, in honor of BREA&D's new Chew-Chew account.

The agency staff had been rehearsed in their roles well into the night, the account supervisor timing each part with a stopwatch. The charts were pinned to the walls, the layouts propped on their easels. A secretary appeared at the door and announced, "Mr. Iscariot, the clients are here." Everyone took seats. The presentation was on.

One by one the ad automatons recited their pitches, displayed the comp ads, played audition commercials, pointed at charts. The clients squirmed. There was much clearing of throats, awkward smiles of feigned approval, restless fingers tapping doomsday beats on the shiny teakwood table. And all mouths chewed their Chew-Chew.

Iscariot sensed the Buferoon account was as good as gone. He stood. "Gentlemen, that concludes our presentation." Where was the rabbit he could pull from his sleeve? "But before we open it up for discussion, I would like to show you one more concept." He unsnapped his attaché case and girded himself to read the Jesus ad: "A KIND WORD ABOUT BAYER ASPIRIN FROM THE MAKERS OF BUFEROON." As he read the copy, the Buferoon product manager leaned forward in rapt amazement, the marketing director wrote furiously, and the ad manager listened slack-jawed. When Iscariot read the line, "We're an honest product, and we think our advertising should be, too," the clients whispered among themselves.

"Well, gentlemen," Iscariot said after he had concluded. "What do you think?"

The Buferoon product manager stood. "That," he exulted, "is absolutely brilliant." The clients loudly applauded.

The BREA&D account team exchanged looks of disbelief. Judas saves the day, saves the account. But Judas knew it was the upstart Jesus who did the saving. Judas gave him a call.

The agency celebration that night was a rollicking event. Judas shared with his colleagues that it was not he who had conceived the daring new concept, but a job applicant trying to prove his mettle. "The reason I took credit for the idea," explained Judas, "was because I felt my experience would lend credibility to the concept."

Jesus was the guest of honor at the agency victory party. The art directors prepared a banner to greet their new hero, the mysterious copywriter job applicant who had saved the Buferoon account. JESUS SAVES proclaimed the banner in Buferoon-blue.

In the weeks to follow Jesus showed remarkable skills in overseeing the development of the multi-media Buferoon concept. He won the respect and approval of all who worked with him. The honest man wrote a whole series of Buferoon ads complimenting, even lauding, Buferoon's competitors. The ads were rich with facts describing how this product or that product had a particular characteristic or advantage, and encouraged the reader to make a selective judgment as to which brand would best suit his needs.

Simple honesty; gentle, understated persuasion; deference and respect for the consumer. Those were the special qualities which made Jesus' ads so disarming. The TV commercials were stunning in their simple restraint. In one, the camera focused on a falling leaf. A gentle breeze lifted it into the sky where it performed an aerial ballet against the clouds to Bach's Prelude and Fugue Number Two in C minor. The closing words on the screen: THIS MOMENT OF PEACE FROM BUFEROON.

When the campaign broke—Buferoon broke the bank. An editorial in the *New York Times* was headlined—HONESTY IS THE BEST GIMMICK. Jesus became a national folk hero overnight and the skyrocketing sales of Buferoon were charted in exponential increments. Advertisers across the land copied the technique. Kindness, gentle honesty and full disclosure became all the rage.

Product after product stood up before the TV screen and shamelessly confessed their past muddled half-truths. Of course, the motivation was still avarice and the goal was share of market. But the more honest they got, the more stuff they sold. Coke confessed its calories; Del Monte produced a riotous taste test commercial comparing their canned peaches to Libby's. Del Monte lost. The closing scene had the Del Monte announcer shrugging his shoulders and stating, "You can't win 'em all." Sea & Ski did an ad on the perils of too much sun.

All across the land raged the great corporate confessional. The more they bared their sins, the more the sales rolled in. Detroit, in a frenzy of automotive catharsis, pledged to right its wrongs. The bucks rolled in to those who followed the fad. But while fads are apt to fade, this fad continued to flourish.

The legend, Jesus, soon became the creative director of BREA&D, overseeing the overhaul of every account in the agency. In an early memo he announced to his staff, "No more braggadocio, weasels, puffery or half-truths in BREA&D ads."

If imitation is the highest flattery, Jesus must have felt complimented indeed, because the new technique became so imitated that it became the standard. The new widespread trust in advertising and advertisers generated increased purchases of virtually all goods and services. The GNP soared as never before, creating millions of new jobs, securing the economy and giving Americans and the whole world a new confidence and exhilaration.

What if Jesus had been born in your generation instead of the year one? In Brooklyn instead of Bethlehem? And what if his father Joseph had been a copywriter instead of a carpenter? Perhaps then, Jesus would have apprenticed for another trade.

But when he put down his hammer, spokeshave and awl and said goodbye to his family and walked out into the world, did he not initiate the greatest advertising campaign the world has ever known? Admittedly, he had an advantage which many ad men don't have today. His product was NEW. And it certainly was AMAZING! But he had other advantages: a curious wisdom, a burning intent; an unshakable spirit; a respect, indeed a love, of his fellow man; the insight to follow his very own star; and the courage to take the risks. He had no budget, a tough sell and a deadly competitor. But he had eloquence, conviction and faith. And his miracle campaign has endured as none other in the history of time.

Christ, what an ad man he was!

INDEX